Peter

PLAYS

Peter Gill was born in 1939 in Cardiff and started his
professional career as an actor. A director as well as a
writer, he has directed over eighty productions in the
UK, Europe and North America. At the Royal Court
Theatre in the sixties, he was responsible for introducing
D. H. Lawrence's plays to the theatre. The founding
director of Riverside Studios and the Royal National
Theatre Studio, Peter Gill lives in London. His plays
include *The Sleepers Den* (Royal Court, London, 1965),
Over Gardens Out (Royal Court, London, 1968), *Small
Change* (Royal Court, London, 1976), *Kick for Touch*
(Royal National Theatre, London, 1983), *Cardiff East*
(Royal National Theatre, London, 1997), *Certain Young
Men* (Almeida Theatre, 1999) and *The York Realist*
(English Touring Theatre, 2001).

PETER GILL

Plays One

The Sleepers Den
Over Gardens Out
Small Change
Kick for Touch
Mean Tears
In the Blue

Introduced by
John Burgess

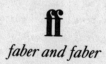

faber and faber

This collection first published in 2002
by Faber and Faber Limited
3 Queen Square London WC1N 3AU
Published in the United States by Faber and Faber Inc.
an affiliate of Farrar, Straus and Giroux LLC, New York

Typeset by Country Setting, Kingsdown, Kent CT14 8ES
Printed in England by Mackays of Chatham plc, Chatham, Kent

The Sleepers Den first published in 1970
by Calder and Boyars Limited © Peter Gill, 1970
Over Gardens Out first published in 1970
by Calder and Boyars Limited © Peter Gill, 1970
Small Change first published in 1985
by Marion Boyars Publishers Ltd © Peter Gill, 1985
Kick for Touch first published in 1985
by Marion Boyars Publishers Ltd © Peter Gill, 1985
In the Blue first published in 1987
by Oberon Books Limited © Peter Gill, 1987
Mean Tears first published in 1987
by Oberon Books Limited © Peter Gill, 1987
This collection © Peter Gill, 2002

A CIP record for this book is available from the British Library

0-571-21238-7

2 4 6 8 10 9 7 5 3 1

Contents

Introduction

> After your death you were better have a bad
> epitaph, than their ill-report while you live.
>
> *Hamlet*, II, ii

It sometimes seems as if Peter Gill's plays are one of the best kept secrets of the British theatre. If the subject comes up in a group of actors, writers, designers or directors, everyone turns out to have their own particular favourite. For some it's the passionate rivalry between the two brothers in *Kick for Touch*; for others it's Mrs Harte and Mrs Driscoll dancing together in *Small Change*; or Julian in *Mean Tears* asking restlessly, 'Is this shirt OK?'; or the three generations of women nested in bed together in *The Sleepers Den*; or the two boys perched on the window sill with the evening light behind them in *Over Gardens Out*; or Michael's explanation of the world in *Cardiff East*. The experiences differ but are linked by their intensity and by a strong sense of personal connection.

> Here goes another day. Let's get 'em all out of it.
> Let's have a sit down. That's the way I think. It's
> wrong I know. And when they're gone, I get lonely.
> But as soon as they're in again, I think, Oh, Christ,
> why don't you all go out and leave me alone.
>
> Mrs Harte, *Small Change*

Part of the plays' intimate appeal lies in their sense of people coping, not in some sentimental put-upon way, but simply getting through the day, managing, making the best of things – the dailiness of life in the enormous complexity of actual living. Some of what is to be coped with is external – joblessness, lack of money or social opportunity – but perhaps the greater struggle is with emotions: fears, obsessions, needs and inherited demands.

> Oh Mrs Harte, I felt as if I didn't exist. I kept looking out of the window but I couldn't work out how it could be possible. It's easy to say so now because although I think it I don't feel it, if you can take my meaning. And the line and the line post and everything. Well the truth to tell I got very frightened, so I locked the bedroom door and I lay down on the bed. Mrs Driscoll, *Small Change*

Side by side with those characters who are managing to cope (more or less) are a group of others who are disintegrating or have disintegrated – Mrs Driscoll in *Small Change*, Shirley in *Cardiff East*, Mrs Shannon in *The Sleepers Den*. One of the characteristics of this writing is the ability to enter the personality of someone who is falling apart. This delineation of extreme psychic frailty helps give Gill's work its particular tone and the presence of such frailty in the plays is like an undertow, which exerts its pull on all but the most robust characters. Sometimes Nature herself seems to share this feeling. Gerard in *Small Change* looks out of the train and sees 'field after field after field, all shaking with nerves'.

VINCENT You ought to be a Catholic.

GERARD I would be if I wasn't one.

Gill's Catholic upbringing also brings its flavour to the writing. It shows not just in the characters' social and ethical concerns but in their wit, their repartee, and their refusal to let each other have the last word. (It was after all the Catholic Church which invented the position of the Devil's advocate to ensure that the opposing viewpoint could be fully dramatised.)

Dear Daddy, I hope you are well, that you are in good health and that it's all right where you are. Dear Daddy, I wish you were home. Dear Daddy, I wish you could come home for good. I hope I'll get another postcard again. We all got our cards and we hope you got ours. Lots of love, your son till death – John Vincent O'Driscoll.

Vincent, Small Change

From little Maria in *The Sleepers Den* hiding behind her comic to escape her mother's growing distress to Anne-Marie and Ryan in *Cardiff East* who take refuge next door to get away from their parents' quarrels, Gill's plays are full of children. Just as there is a strong sense of the adult characters having had parents (and having to deal with what the parents handed down to them), so Gill is careful to show how present entanglements have their impact on the next generation. From the teenagers in *Over Gardens Out* to the quite small babies in *Cardiff East*, Gill shows childhood as a vortex of adult emotions, anxiety, sexual possessiveness, obsession, terror, seduction and moments of sheer weightless bliss.

Whose face did my grin start on? On whose face will it end?

Gerard, Small Change

This strong feeling of connection between generations means that Gill is often writing what are in effect history plays (though not in any fashionable sense). The presence of history is perhaps most overt in *Cardiff East*, which as its title suggests takes a place and shows us a group of people living there – pensioners, forty-somethings, twenty-somethings, teenagers, school-age children and babes in arms – everyone with their different aspirations and experiences of the world. On one level, history for these characters has been reduced to material for a pub quiz – 'Alfred Sisley was married in Cardiff' – but on another level history is the very fabric of people's lives. The sense of time and community is overwhelming. *Small Change* tries to chart a connection between the immediate post war and the revolutionary hopes of the late sixties and early seventies; *Mean Tears* catches perfectly the mixture of heartlessness, self-obsession and despair that characterised the late 1980s. In each of these plays Gill includes characters (Michael, Gerard, Stephen) who as well as living the experience are also trying to interpret it and give it an intellectual dimension.

> He is concerned with the whole of life since the particular is unsatisfying – with the particular because the whole of life cannot be focused into vividness.   William Gerhardie on Chekhov

The three godparents that stand behind these plays are Anton Chekhov, D. H. Lawrence and Samuel Beckett. Gill has long had a particular affection for Beckett (especially the short works such as *Eh Joe*, *Play* and *All That Fall*); his second play *A Provincial Life* is based on and extrapolated from a Chekhov short story, and his version of *The Cherry Orchard* is the best rendering of Chekhov into English that there is, capturing perfectly the sense of Mayakovsky's remark that 'Chekhov's language is as precise as "Hello" and as simple as "Give me a glass of tea";' and of course his production of the three Lawrence plays at the Royal Court Theatre in 1968 is now legendary. But it is the combination of the three influences that is so creatively interesting. Imagine Beckett and Chekhov without Lawrence, or Lawrence and Beckett without Chekhov, and the mixture is immediately less vivifying.

> Whether I shall turn out to be the hero of my own life or whether that station will be held by anybody else, these pages must show.
>   Charles Dickens, *David Copperfield*

The desire to put the ordinary centre stage and in doing so to rescue it from the condescension of the cultured classes was shared by many theatre artists in the period after the war – and not just at the Royal Court Theatre. Joan Littlewood's actors returning from active service couldn't see why they had to revert to playing comic servants on the fringes of middle-class plays and set out to create work in which they would have the leading roles. In the same way Mrs Harte and Mrs Driscoll are two 'ordinary' Cardiff housewives yet they stand – like Hamlet – at the centre of their own consciousness and that of the play.

> I want to paint men and women with that something
> of the eternal, which the halo used to symbolise,
> and which we seek to convey by the actual radiance
> and vibration of our colouring.   Vincent Van Gogh

It is natural for the painter to speak of the 'vibration of our colouring' but for the playwright it is not pigment but dialogue that has to be full of vibration. Gill's dialogue is unhurried, witty, faithful to the moment, yet capable of great lyric power. His writing has as its defining qualities a refusal to over-dramatise and a way of never looking at life as if it were only a problem. His work at its best creates the sensation that what is being conveyed is not some idea (still less some abstract theory) about experience but simply and directly experience itself.

John Burgess

THE SLEEPERS DEN

The Sleepers Den in an earlier version was presented by the English Stage Society at the Royal Court Theatre on Sunday 28 February 1965, with the following cast:

Old Mrs Shannon Kathleen Williams
Maria Jean Woollard
Mrs Shannon Eileen Atkins
Mr Blake Anthony Hall
Frankie Trevor Peacock
Mary Lynch Sonia Graham

Directed by Desmond O'Donovan

The present version was first presented in the Theatre Upstairs at the Royal Court Theatre on 18 November 1969, with the following cast:

Old Mrs Shannon Madeline Thomas
Maria Kimberly Iles
Mrs Shannon Eileen Atkins
Mr Blake Anthony Douse
Frankie John Rees
Mary Lynch Margaret John

Directed by Peter Gill
Designed by Deirdre Clancy

Characters

Old Mrs Shannon
Maria
Mrs Shannon
Mr Blake
Frankie
Mary Lynch

Act One

A bed centre. Door left to the back kitchen. Door right to the passage and the front door. Table and chairs. A sideboard. An armchair near the foot of the bed.
   Old Mrs Shannon in bed. Maria sitting down reading a comic. Mrs Shannon whistling in the back kitchen.

Maria Nana's crying.

   Enter Mrs Shannon.

Mrs Shannon What are you crying for? What? You are, Mama. Just because of that. You are, I can see you are. Here you are. There's a silly.

   They both laugh.

Maria Oh, don't laugh at her.

Mrs Shannon She's laughing. That's better. You're a proper baby, eh? She's meant to be the baby. You've been asleep nearly all day.

Old Mrs Shannon I wants some tea, Joannie.

Mrs Shannon Mama, I made you some. It went cold.

Old Mrs Shannon Tea.

Mrs Shannon Alright. Stay there. I'll put the kettle on in a minute.

Old Mrs Shannon Joannie.

Mrs Shannon Mama, I said stay.

Old Mrs Shannon I don't need bed.

Mrs Shannon What do you need? Do you want the toilet?

Old Mrs Shannon No.

Mrs Shannon Now let me know when you do, Mama, not like the last time. Be good now.

Maria You should stay in bed, Nana. You don't like it up.

Old Mrs Shannon Shut up, you. It's not for you to say.

Mrs Shannon Now, Mama, come on or you won't get your tea.

Maria Oh, is she staring? Get back to bed, go on.

Mrs Shannon Shut up, you.

Maria Well, I don't want her up.

Mrs Shannon It's a pity for you. It's hard lines on you.

Maria I'm going out.

Mrs Shannon Hey.

Maria What?

Mrs Shannon Maria.

Maria What?

Mrs Shannon Don't you come in here late.

Maria I'm going upstairs, you don't mind? (*Exits.*)

Mrs Shannon Come on now, into bed.

Old Mrs Shannon Stop ordering me about. I'm staying here.

Mrs Shannon Mama, I'm tired. You get in and then I can make some tea.

Old Mrs Shannon I've no need to be in bed.

Mrs Shannon I know, but I'm tired.

Old Mrs Shannon Why did you put me there?

Mrs Shannon All those weeks, why didn't you get up?

Old Mrs Shannon That's different.

Mrs Shannon Well, you're going now.

Old Mrs Shannon mutters.

What? What did you say. Why do you talk under your breath as if you was afraid for me to hear? Why do you always pretend I'm going to do something to you? I could kill you when you do that.

Old Mrs Shannon mutters.

Talk out loud. Will you. Look. Look, if I give you a drink, will you take a couple of tablets I got? Make you have a sleep.

Old Mrs Shannon Leave off.

Mrs Shannon You're going to. Come on, Mama.

Old Mrs Shannon What? What? I'll tell Frank I've been living on them tablets.

Mrs Shannon You do and I'll tell him about what you did last night. Do you hear?

Old Mrs Shannon What did I do? I don't know.

Mrs Shannon You do. You tell him and that'll be it, I'm telling you. Stand up. Stop it will you, Mama. Don't go like that.

Knock at the front door. Old Mrs Shannon jumps.

Old Mrs Shannon What's that? What's that?

9

Mrs Shannon Shut up. I'm not in. Shhh.

Old Mrs Shannon Frankie?

Mrs Shannon It's the club man. I can't pay them. Shut up, will you. (*She takes the club book and hides it in her pocket.*)

Old Mrs Shannon I'm going to bed.

Mrs Shannon You're not. Shut up. (*She goes to the door.*) Who left the door open?

Mr Blake Mrs Shannon. I know you're in, you know. The front door is open. I'm afraid you must answer.

Mrs Shannon (*to her mother*) Have you been opening the door?

Maria (*off*) Mama, there's someone at the door.

Mrs Shannon Our Maria. I'll kill her. (*to her mother*) Get out there. Go on . . . out there. I won't be long.

    Knock.

Mr Blake, is it?

Mr Blake That's the name.

Mrs Shannon Look. There's a sweet out there for you. Go on. I'll be a minute.

    Old Mrs Shannon goes into the back kitchen.

Listen, Mr Blake. I'm sorry I can't ask you in but my mother, I'm trying to get her tidied up. Oh, come in, Mr Blake.

    Enter Mr Blake.

I'm sorry I'm looking like this. You'll have to excuse me.

Mr Blake Don't worry, you ladies have to work. Don't mind me. How is your mother? I hear you have an invalid on your hands.

Mrs Shannon Who said that?

Mr Blake I asked Reg Cottrell when I visited him in hospital about his old round.

Mrs Shannon Oh yes. How is Mr Cottrell? When's he coming back?

Mr Blake Oh, not yet. Not yet.

Mrs Shannon Oh.

Mr Blake He's quite comfortable, they say.

Mrs Shannon They always say that.

Mr Blake Well, Mrs Shannon. Let's get this cleared up a bit, shall we? (*opening his account book*)

Mrs Shannon I thought I'd wait for Mr Cottrell.

Old Mrs Shannon (*from the back kitchen*) Joan. I want to come in.

Mrs Shannon You stay there.

Old Mrs Shannon Joan.

Mrs Shannon Stay there.

Old Mrs Shannon Is that Mr Cottrell?

Mrs Shannon I'm sorry. Stay out there, I said. I said I wouldn't be long. Well, Mr Blake, I thought I'd wait . . .

Old Mrs Shannon (*enters*) Is that Mr Cottrell?

Mrs Shannon Mama!

Old Mrs Shannon Don't shut me up. That's not Mr Cottrell.

Mr Blake No. No.

She gets into bed.

Mrs Shannon Go on then. Now I'm talking. Mind!

Mr Blake A bit of a worry?

Mrs Shannon No.

Mr Blake Well, Mrs Shannon, let's make up your book.

Mrs Shannon Well, the trouble is, Mr Blake, I just can't put my hands on it. I've looked everywhere. I'll come across it, mind. Is it alright next week?

Mr Blake You know, Mrs Shannon, this is the eighth week.

Mrs Shannon Is it? Are you sure?

Mr Blake Yes, Mrs Shannon, and it isn't alright next week. It's only Mr Cottrell's going into hospital and the extra work entailed that's stopped Mr Blakey having something done about it. You know what I mean?

Mrs Shannon Well, Mr Cottrell knows I'll pay.

Mr Blake I know, Mrs Shannon, but I've got to take the rap for this street now and I haven't been with the firm long.

Mrs Shannon Well, I haven't got it, Mr Blake.

Mr Blake When does your husband come in, Mrs Shannon?

Mrs Shannon I haven't got a husband.

Mr Blake I think I really ought to have a word . . .

Mrs Shannon I haven't got a husband.

Mr Blake Oh, I'm sorry, I didn't know you were widowed.

Mrs Shannon I'm not. Don't be sorry. You could speak to my brother only he's out. Mr Blake, I'm glad to tell you the truth. I'd be grateful if you didn't try and get hold of him. It's my doing getting into this debt. I suppose I can't borrow any more off you?

Mr Blake Now, Mrs Shannon! I don't know what to do, Mrs Shannon, for the best. Apart from the clothing balance, there's the money lent . . . the loan and the interest. I don't know I'm sure. I'm afraid the firm might have to take action.

Mrs Shannon Have a heart, Mr Blake.

Mr Blake It's not a matter of heart, Mrs Shannon. It's my job. Perhaps Mr Blakey will come himself and have a chat.

Mrs Shannon I might have it next week.

Mr Blake I'll tell him. I don't know what good it will do, mind. He was pretty firm.

Mrs Shannon I might have it next week.

Mr Blake Well, I've got the rest of the street to do. I haven't got the hang of it yet.

Mrs Shannon OK, Mr Blake.

Mr Blake Don't come out.

Mrs Shannon No. It's no bother.

Mr Blake Bye. Bye. (*to her mother*) Goodbye, Mrs . . .

Mrs Shannon Shannon.

Mr Blake Bye. Bye, then. (*Exits.*)

Old Mrs Shannon I'd rather Mr Cottrell.

Mrs Shannon Well, you can't have him, he's in hospital.

Old Mrs Shannon Who is he?

Mrs Shannon I don't know.

Old Mrs Shannon I'm awful tired.

Mrs Shannon Well, if you're tired, why are you always getting out of bed? You don't know what you're doing half the time.

She gets her club book and looks at it and then puts it away. Her mother gets out of bed.

Come on now, stay there. Come on now. Stop it, do you hear, stop. I'm sick of it!

Old Mrs Shannon shouts.

I'm not touching you now, am I? Bugger you, shut up. I'm not going to hurt you. You'll have them in from next door. I didn't hit you. I didn't hit you, you bugger. You bugger, I will hit you. Keep still, I will. You bugger, I will. I will. I'll kill you. God'll have you one day for this. Keep quiet now. Now get in there. You can't meet people looking like that. Look, Mama, let me wash you and then we'll have some people in to see you. Come on now. (*Exits and brings back a bottle of tablets.*) Have one of these.

Frankie with his bike.

Who's that now?

Mrs Shannon Is that you, Frank?

Frankie It's me.

Mrs Shannon Come on now.

Mother is docile.

Now remember what I said. (*putting tablets in her pocket*)

Old Mrs Shannon Frank.

Mrs Shannon Just you keep that shut. (*pointing to her own mouth*)

Enter Frankie.

You're in early.

Frankie Meaning I'm what?

Mrs Shannon How many did you have?

Frankie How many?

Mrs Shannon Come off it, Frankie. Down the Trafalgar, after work.

Frankie Where's the grub then?

Mrs Shannon Alright. Sit down before you fall down.

Frankie Have you ever seen me otherwise than straight sober?

Mrs Shannon Ha. Ha. (*Exits into the kitchen.*)

Frankie (*to his mother*) How are you? Come on then. (*tucking her in*) What's for tea?

Mrs Shannon Bread and lard.

Frankie That'll be your cards for you if it is. Who was that fellow at the door?

Mrs Shannon What?

Frankie One of the club men. Was it?

Mrs Shannon Yes. How do you know?

Frankie I saw him turn the corner. (*Pause.*) Alright?

Mrs Shannon Aye.

Maria enters with a comic, walks to table, sits.

Frankie Hiya, I thought you were out on the street – give us that after you.

Maria Go on, you got the *Echo*.

Frankie So I have. Ahhhh. (*Stretches. Pause.*) Aye, did I tell you about my dream, Joannie?

Mrs Shannon What?

Frankie The dream I had last night.

Mrs Shannon What dream?

Frankie I had this dream and I woke up and it went on going.

Maria How could it go on?

Mrs Shannon And?

Frankie It went on. I was sitting up. I can't remember it really. Something. About these three women. Three women. And three pains.

Maria What were they like?

Frankie Well, that's it.

Maria What?

Frankie They were the three women who works in the coffee tavern down the docks. Aye.

Maria I've had better dreams than that. (*Goes back to comic.*)

Frankie Well, you would.

Mrs Shannon (*enters with his food*) Here we are, come on, Frankie.

Frankie Alright.

Tea poured for the four of them.

Old Mrs Shannon Have you made the tea?

Frankie Oh, you pipes up for the tea.

Mrs Shannon Yes, here you are. Tea tank.

Frankie I don't know what your guts must be like.

Silence. Eating. Frankie eats piggishly.

Mrs Shannon Don't make so much noise, Frankie. There's a good boy.

Frankie What are you talking about. I got to eat, haven't I?

Mrs Shannon Not as loud as you.

Pause. She exits. Noise from the kitchen.

Frankie Any more tea? (*Pause.*) Any more tea?

Mrs Shannon (*off*) Have a look in the pot.

Frankie No.

Mrs Shannon (*off*) I'll fill it up.

She enters.

You don't half bolt your food. (*She takes the teapot up.*)

Frankie Aye. God. I hates food. Bloody disgusting. You should have seen the people in the café dinner time. Full up to their heads. Hey, our Joan, got anything for afters?

Mrs Shannon No. Some biscuits out here if you want some.

Frankie No.

Mother snores.

She's dozed off.

Mrs Shannon You going out?

Frankie Expect so.

Mrs Shannon Never in, are you?

Frankie What's Mama been like?

Mrs Shannon Quiet really. Give us that. There was a big mouse on the draining board just now. He came out of that panel.

Frankie You want to get it seen to.

Mrs Shannon Yes.

Exit Maria.

Give us that. (*She clears his plate, exits.*)

Frankie goes to his mother.

Frankie Alright? (*She is awake.*) OK today? What happened, anything? (*sitting on the bed*) What do you want? What, love? Aah. (*He goes away.*)

Old Mrs Shannon Cupboard.

Frankie What do you want? What?

Old Mrs Shannon It's the cupboard.

Frankie What's in the cupboard?

Old Mrs Shannon In it. There.

Frankie This right?

Old Mrs Shannon Not that.

Frankie But you pointed here. Where? This it? (*He takes out a bottle.*)

Old Mrs Shannon No, that.

Frankie Do you have a drink of this?

Old Mrs Shannon No. Don't like it. Joan does. But only sometimes. Put it back.

Frankie Hey, Joan.

Mrs Shannon What?

Frankie Do you give this to our Mama?

Mrs Shannon (*enters*) What?

Frankie This.

Mrs Shannon Yes. Well, you know we got her some tonic wine before.

Frankie I know. This isn't it.

Mrs Shannon It's made by the monks that is. Buckfast Tonic Wine.

Old Mrs Shannon That's right, the monks make it.

Frankie We finished that bottle.

Mrs Shannon We got it in a club.

Frankie You didn't tell me.

Mrs Shannon I don't have to put everything down, do I? Do you want me to present bills? Do you? On what you brings home. It's a tonic.

Frankie I just haven't noticed you give her one, that's all.

Mrs Shannon So. You don't have sight in here half the time, do you?

Frankie Well, what's it in there for?

Mrs Shannon Where do you expect me to keep it, in the bloody outside dub for your inspection?

Frankie But you keeps clothes and that in here.

Mrs Shannon I know.

Frankie Well, what's it in there for?

Mrs Shannon (*sarcastically*) I'm being tidy.

Frankie Well, it's time someone was. Look at it. What does it look like?

Mrs Shannon I looks at nothing else.

Frankie Whose bloody fault is that? How much was it, then?

Mrs Shannon How should I know?

Frankie Well, how should *I* know? How should *I* know?

Mrs Shannon I got it on a club.

Frankie Oh.

Pause. He looks at the bottle. She doesn't take it.

Must have cost something. (*He goes into the back kitchen to wash.*)

Mrs Shannon I'll pay you out.

Old Mrs Shannon What?

Mrs Shannon Don't come it. I'll get you. You wait.

Old Mrs Shannon You won't.

Mrs Shannon Won't I? We'll see. We'll just see.

Old Mrs Shannon You'd better not that's all.

Mrs Shannon And what can you do?

Enter Frankie. He goes upstairs.

Here, I bought these and you take 'em. Go on. I don't care. Shout. Go on. (*Gives her the two tablets.*) Now let's have a bit of peace.

She looks at the bottle and then puts it away. Knock at the front door.

Who the hell is that now? I'll go!

She goes to the door. It is Mary Lynch.

Mary Hello.

Mrs Shannon Good evening.

Mary I'm from the Legion of Mary.

Mrs Shannon Oh yes.

Mary I've come to see Mrs Shannon.

Mrs Shannon Oh. Come in, will you. Mind the bike.

Mary Lynch knocks herself on it.

I'm sorry. There's nowhere else we've got to put it.

Enter.

Mary Is it you I've come to see?

Mrs Shannon I expect it's my mother. She's going off to sleep.

Mary Oh, you've got someone in bed. I hope I'm not disturbing her.

Mrs Shannon No, it's alright.

Mary I don't live in this parish, of course. So we've never met. But I belong to the Legion down here. Do you know about our work?

Mrs Shannon Oh yes.

Mary Well, in our meeting last week we heard that Mrs Shannon wasn't well. So that's why I'm here. We usually work in twos.

Mrs Shannon That's right.

Mary I was really meant to come with a friend of mine. Eileen Dwyer. Do you know her? She lives over here. Well over the black bridge actually. Edward's Terrace that was. Do you know them?

Mrs Shannon Can't say I do. But I don't go over there very often.

Mary Well, she's got a cold coming, I think.

Mrs Shannon That's nasty.

Mary There's so many about. That's why I've popped in on my own.

Mrs Shannon Would you like to sit down?

Mary Thanks. (*She sits.*)

Mrs Shannon Shall I wake her up?

Mary No, please don't do that. How is she? Do you have to stay with her all the time?

Mrs Shannon Not all. But I don't go out much.

Mary I suppose you're very busy with the housework.

Mrs Shannon It's not very tidy.

Mary It's not criticism, believe me. I hardly do any at all.

Mrs Shannon Yes, I get very nervy.

Mary That's awful, I believe.

Mrs Shannon It isn't very pleasant.

Mary I believe you have to fight it.

Mrs Shannon Yes, you do.

Mary I could sit with you a little if you liked.

Mrs Shannon I'm alright I assure you. I'll make a cup of tea if you like.

Mary No, Mrs Shannon. I just called to see Mrs Shannon to see if we could be of help as far as the church is concerned.

Mrs Shannon Won't you have one? I'd put the kettle on.

Mary Thank you.

She goes out. Noise.

Mrs Shannon. Does this mean you never go out?

Mrs Shannon I said sometimes.

Enter Mrs Shannon.

Mary Perhaps I might suggest . . .

Mrs Shannon Don't ask me to do anything now. I'm not up to it really.

Mary A young woman like you.

Mrs Shannon I couldn't really. I just go round the shop. I'm not really up to it, see.

Mary Oh, I'm sorry, I didn't know you were ill.

Mrs Shannon I'm not.

Mary Does Mrs Shannon get the sacraments?

Mrs Shannon Not any more.

Mary Would you like me to arrange it?

Mrs Shannon No. I don't think so.

Mary I could.

Mrs Shannon No. (*dreamily*) We haven't seen a priest for, oo, must be a twelvemonth.

Mary Do you really mean it? Not even to bring communion to your mother?

Mrs Shannon Not since, oo, must be Easter twelve-month. I shouldn't think she'd be allowed now.

Mary Oh I don't know.

Mrs Shannon Well, look at her.

Mary Do you want me to find out?

Mrs Shannon No, don't bother.

Mary No bother.

Mrs Shannon You've got other things to do I'm sure.

Mary I would, you know.

Mrs Shannon No. Thanks.

Maria (*off*) Mama.

Mrs Shannon That's my little girl.

Mary Oh, I thought you were in by yourself. Does she go to a Catholic school?

Mrs Shannon Oh yes. Of course.

Maria enters.

Maria Can I have a drink of water?

Mrs Shannon There's a tap out there. She goes on Sundays.

Mary That's good.

Maria Mama?

Mrs Shannon What? Don't whine, Maria, you're not a baby, in front of people. What do you want now?

Mary Hello.

Mrs Shannon Come on now, Maria, be your age.

Mary Do you enjoy school?

Mrs Shannon Alright.

Mary What's your best subject?

Maria I dunno.

Mary Have you made your first communion?

Maria Of course.

Mary Of course. Well then, what month is this?

Maria Month? October I suppose.

Mary What month is it though?

Maria What month? I said.

Mary What do we know it as?

Maria Oh. We. 'The month of the Holy Rosary.'

Mary Have you got a rosary?

Maria Nana has one on the bed. Look at that.

Mrs Shannon That's mother-of-pearl.

Mary That's nice. Do you ever say it? It's the month you know, for saying it. In church we say it every night. Some people even say the Rosary at home. The Family Rosary. I don't wish to be rude, but might I suggest we might say a decade now? For your mother. Families often say the Rosary together you know.

Mrs Shannon What now?

Mary Would you mind?

Mrs Shannon Here?

Mary Why not?

25

Mrs Shannon What about my brother? He's upstairs.

Mary Oh. Would he mind?

Mrs Shannon I haven't got one.

Mary Please borrow mine.

Mrs Shannon No, that's yours.

Maria I'm going out, Mama.

Mrs Shannon Stay here, you little cat.

Maria I don't want to.

Mary I'm sure Our Lady would be hurt to hear you say that.

They kneel around the bed.

Shall we take the joyful mysteries, and this is the first decade, the Annunciation. In this we contemplate the Annunciation to Our Lady by the Angel Gabriel of the birth of Our Blessed Lord.

A decade of the Rosary.* The Sign of the Cross. Our Father. Ten Hail Marys. One Glory Be to The Father. The child fidgets occasionally through it. Sometimes Old Mrs Shannon snores. In the middle Frankie enters.

Frankie Joan, I'm off. Oh.

Mary I'm so sorry.

Frankie That's alright.

Mary I came to visit your mother actually.

Frankie Why don't you wake her up?

Mary No, please.

Frankie You from church?

26

Mary Yes. Actually I'm visiting from the Legion of Mary.

Frankie I didn't know we had a visitor expected.

Mrs Shannon This is my brother Francis.

Frankie Francis? Pleased to meet you.

Mary You going out?

Frankie I was just off.

Mary Oh. Well, it was nice to have met you.

Frankie Trying to get rid of me?

Mary Oh, sorry, I thought you were going.

Frankie I'm sorry we don't have anything to offer you. Unless there is anything in the cupboard. Joan'll make you a cup of tea.

Mrs Shannon I am.

---

* *A Decade of the Rosary*

Sign of the Cross In the name of The Father, and of The Son, and of The Holy Ghost. Amen.

Our Father Our Father who art in heaven, hallowed be Thy Name. Thy kingdom come, Thy will be done on earth as it is in heaven. Give us this day our daily bread and forgive us our trespasses as we forgive them who trespass against us, and lead us not into temptation, but deliver us from evil. Amen.

Hail Mary Hail Mary full of grace, the Lord is with thee. Blessed art thou among women and blessed is the fruit of thy womb, Jesus. Holy Mary, Mother of God, pray for us sinners, now and at the hour of our death. Amen.

Glory Be to The Father Glory be to The Father and to The Son, and to The Holy Ghost, as it was in the beginning, is now and ever shall be, world without end. Amen.

Frankie Tra, then, I'll be going.

Mary Goodnight.

Frankie exits.

Mrs Shannon In and out. He's just had his tea.

Mary Perhaps he's got an appointment.

Mrs Shannon I wouldn't know. It won't be long, the tea. Here's your rosary.

Mary Oh thank you.

Mrs Shannon Maria, put your Nana's back.

Mary Aren't we going to finish our prayers?

Mrs Shannon Maria.

Maria Oh, Mama. (*putting it back*)

Mrs Shannon Back.

Mary I do think it would be nice if we could finish them.

Maria I'm going out again now.

Mrs Shannon Not now.

Mary Late to be out.

Mrs Shannon She's not going. It's nearly time for bed.

Mary Is it her bedtime? I mustn't keep you. Where's my bag?

Mrs Shannon I didn't mean that.

Mary No, really. I ought to go. My mother doesn't know I'm out.

Maria gives her her handbag. With it is a black mantilla.

Maria That's nice, isn't it?

Mary Do you like it? That's my mantilla.

Maria I know. People wear them in church.

Mary That's right. I've just been to Benediction. I got it when I went on a holiday in Spain.

Maria My friend got one like that, brought back for her.

Mrs Shannon Thanks for calling, then.

Mary That's alright. I hope your mother will be better.

Mrs Shannon There's nothing wrong with her really. I keep her there. It keeps her quiet.

Mary Well, really, I must go.

Mrs Shannon Say ta ta, Maria.

Mary Bye bye, love. (*Exits.*)

Mrs Shannon Can you see?

Mary (*off*) Oh yes.

Mrs Shannon Good night then.

Exits. Mrs Shannon comes back in. Pause. She sits.

Oh. We forgot the tea. Fancy that.

Mrs Shannon goes out into the kitchen. Maria gets on the bed next to her grandmother, playing with the rosary. Old Mrs Shannon stirs.

Old Mrs Shannon Joan.

Maria She's not here.

Old Mrs Shannon What? You been to church?

Maria What do you mean? Of course I haven't been to church.

Old Mrs Shannon (*puzzled*) Oh. You should go, you know. I feel a bit funny. After Catechism. As I was walking home from church one Sunday afternoon. We dared to cross the feeder, by the floating logs that were in it. The canal under the bridge. I fell in and it was only my hair that saved me. Down to here it was then. It floated out over the top while I was trapped under the logs that closed over me. He pulled me out by my hair and he lent me his coat and we ran all the way down to my mother's.

Maria Did you now?

Old Mrs Shannon What?

Maria Oh nothing. (*putting rosary away*)

Mrs Shannon comes in. She sits down – Maria is walking about. Old Mrs Shannon goes to sleep.

Mammy?

Mrs Shannon What?

Maria Can I go out?

Mrs Shannon No.

Maria Come on, Mam. Mama.

Mrs Shannon No, I said it's too late.

Maria You're mean you are. You are.

Mrs Shannon Be quiet now, Maria. There's a good girl.

Old Mrs Shannon snores.

Listen to her.

Maria tries to get on her mother's lap.

Get off now. (*She's tired.*)

Maria Shall I comb your hair, Nana?

Mrs Shannon Leave her, I've given her a tablet.

Maria Come on, Nana, let me comb your hair?

Mrs Shannon Oh, don't comb her hair this time of night.

Maria Come on, Nana. Where's the comb? Where's the comb, Nana?

Mrs Shannon Look.

Maria Nana. Where's the comb?

Mrs Shannon Look. Look. How should I know? You don't want the comb.

Maria I do. (*She walks about, frustrated.*) Where's Frankie's comb, Mama?

Mrs Shannon Christ, there. There's the comb.

Maria gets the comb.

Maria Haven't we got a better one?

Mrs Shannon Shut up, will you?

Maria Don't fall asleep, Mama. Oh don't go to sleep. (*She goes to the bed. She combs her grandmother's hair.*) There, that's nice. You'll like this. It won't hurt. (*She drags the comb through her hair.*) Keep still. Keep still.

Grandmother cries out. Maria jumps off the bed.

Mrs Shannon See, I told you to leave her alone.

Maria It's not my fault, it's her hair.

Mrs Shannon I told you to leave her alone.

Maria It's knotty.

Mrs Shannon What did you want to do that to her for?

Maria Oh. She doesn't notice. (*She wanders round the room, putting the comb through her own hair.*) Come on, Mama. Mammy, come on, let's comb your hair.

Mrs Shannon Well, no pulling. Do you hear?

The child plays with her mother's hair for a while.

Maria Oh I wish it would go properly. You should have it washed. It'd look much lighter. Nana, look at that. You ought to put more lipstick on, you ought. To make yourself look nicer. You ought to wear stuff on your eyes, Mama. Look in the mirror. Mama.

She pushes her. Her mother has relaxed.

Mama. You're not asleep, Mama. I know you. Oh Mama, have a look. Look at it. Mama. (*She pulls.*) Mama. Oh, Mama, don't do that. Mama, wake up. (*She looks at her mother's eyes, laughing.*) You're having me on again. Look, Mama, Nana's got out of bed. She's going out, Mama. Come on, stop pretending – like you are. Mama.

She pulls her mother's hair. Mrs Shannon sits up.

Mrs Shannon Aye, that hurt, you little mare. What'd you do that for?

Maria You wasn't asleep.

Mrs Shannon I was asleep.

Maria You wasn't. I know you.

Mrs Shannon You know me, do you? I was.

Maria You wasn't.

Mrs Shannon What if I was dead? What would you do then eh? Eh? You'd have something to cry over then, wouldn't you? And what'd you do then?

She pushes her out of the way and goes into the back kitchen. Maria tries to open the door. Mrs Shannon slams it back. Maria pretends not to care. She goes back to it.

Maria Mama, I want to come in. (*She knocks.*) Mam. (*She bangs.*) Let me in, Mammy. Mammy. Mammy. Mammy.

Eventually she stops and walks around the room.
Plays. Goes to her grandmother.

Are you still asleep?

Grandmother stirs.

Come on. (*She goes to the door.*) Well, I'm going upstairs.
I'm going to bed. I'm going up.

She goes upstairs.
Old Mrs Shannon wakes up.

Old Mrs Shannon Joan? (*She goes to the back kitchen.*)

Mrs Shannon (*off*) Get out of here. Mama, don't wake
up now. It's time for bed now.

Old Mrs Shannon I've been asleep.

Mrs Shannon (*off*) I know. Try to go off again. (*Enters.*)

Old Mrs Shannon I can't. I feel sick.

Mrs Shannon I don't know about that. I'm going up to
bed.

Old Mrs Shannon Joan.

Mrs Shannon Now. Now.

Old Mrs Shannon Will you sleep with me down here?

Mrs Shannon Now, Mama, you know how restless I am.

Old Mrs Shannon It's awful cold down here. It is cold.
I'll get to sleep better.

Mrs Shannon Frank'll be in soon. He'll come to see if
you're alright.

Old Mrs Shannon I won't get to sleep. Come on. I'll give
you something.

Mrs Shannon What have you got to give? Oh alright,
but only until you goes to sleep.

Old Mrs Shannon Alright then. Well, get into bed then.

Mrs Shannon undresses and gets into bed.

Mrs Shannon Come on then, Mama, shift over. Oh, you're like ice.

Old Mrs Shannon Well, it is cold down here when the fire goes out.

Mrs Shannon Come on then, *cwtch* up, oh, I forgot the light.

Maria (*off*) Mama?

Mrs Shannon I'm not answering.

Maria Our Mama. Come on up.

Mrs Shannon I thought you'd be going to sleep.

Maria I can't get to sleep.

Mrs Shannon Go on now, I'll be up in a minute.

Maria Come on now.

Old Mrs Shannon She's staying with me.

Mrs Shannon Shut up now.

Enter Maria in her nightdress.

Maria You're a big liar, our Mama. You've got to come to bed.

Mrs Shannon I'm just seeing Nana off to sleep.

Old Mrs Shannon laughs.

Maria Come on, Mammy.

Mrs Shannon Come on, you jealous mare, get in here with us then. (*Pause.*) Come on.

Maria gets in with them.

Old Mrs Shannon There's no room.

Mrs Shannon I know there's no room. Shift over and make room. Now then you two, I wants some quiet out of you now. I'm tired. Get out and put the light out, Maria.

Maria No.

Mrs Shannon Go on.

Maria I'll catch cold.

Mrs Shannon Well, you shouldn't have got up.

Maria puts the light out.

Come on now, Frank'll be in. Did you say your prayers, Maria?

Maria Did you?

Mrs Shannon That's not the point.

Maria You didn't.

Mrs Shannon I did. I said 'em quick. Now go to sleep.

They try and sleep. Eventually Frankie comes in at the front door. Pauses in the hall.

Maria *and* **Mrs Shannon** Shhhh . . .

Frankie You asleep, Mama?

No sound.

You alright? (*Comes into room.*) Should have raked the ashes out. You asleep, our Mama?

Old Mrs Shannon Yes.

Frankie That's alright then.

Maria giggles.

Who's that? Our Maria. Get out. Our Joannie. What are you all doing down here?

Mrs Shannon Don't put the light on, our Frankie.

Light on.

Maria Where have you been, Frankie?

Frankie Mind your own business. You should be in bed.

Mrs Shannon Let's smell your breath. Come here.

Frankie Two pints, that's all I had.

Mrs Shannon Stinking.

Maria You stinks, our Frankie. Where've you been?

Frankie Out.

Maria Where?

Frankie Out.

Mrs Shannon Now you should know better than to ask him.

Frankie Where's the clock, our Joan?

Mrs Shannon On the mantelpiece.

Maria I think he's had one too many.

Frankie I'll give you one too much.

Mrs Shannon Stop it, our Frankie. I'm trying to get them to sleep.

Frankie And you.

Maria Get her, Frankie.

He lifts his sister up. They scream.

Mrs Shannon Francis! You'll frighten our Mam.

Frankie I won't, will I? Come on then. Tuck you up. Alright? You alright? Good night.

Mrs Shannon Put the light out.

Light out.

Frankie, the clock.

Frankie Oh, aye.

Mrs Shannon Wind it.

Frankie Yes. What time shall I set it?

Mrs Shannon What time you on?

Frankie Six to two, starting tomorrow.

Mrs Shannon Better have five-thirty then.

Frankie OK. Goodnight. God bless. Hey, our Joan.

Mrs Shannon Yes?

Frankie Everything alright?

Mrs Shannon What do you mean?

Frankie Today. OK?

Pause.

Mrs Shannon Yea.

Frankie No trouble?

Pause.

Mrs Shannon No.

Frankie Alright then. Goodnight all.

He goes upstairs. Breathing. Movement.

Maria You asleep, Mam? (*Pause.*) Mam?

End of Act One.

Act Two

Later in the week.

Old Mrs Shannon asleep. Mrs Shannon in the armchair. Maria sitting.

Maria Where was I born? (*Pause.*) Mama? Go on. Here was it? Mama? How did it happen? Tell us. Was the nurse late? What about Frankie? Go on, say. You know. How he saw me just after and what did he say. Mean. What was I like?

Mrs Shannon Did you go round Christine's then?

Maria Yes.

Pause.

Mrs Shannon Anyway, I'm not your mother, you know that.

Maria Mama.

Mrs Shannon It's true. I haven't been your mother all these years and I don't know what you're like.

Maria Mama.

Mrs Shannon Don't be so soft.

Maria (*burying herself*) Liar.

Pause.

I think I'll go round Christine's. I said I would.

Mrs Shannon Why don't you wait for her to come round to you? You don't want to run after people, you know. What do you want to wait on her for? You want to look out for yourself.

Maria Oh. How would you know? (*breaking away*)

Mrs Shannon I do know.

Maria You don't know nothing if you ask me. (*Exits.*)

Mrs Shannon tries to settle her mother.

Mrs Shannon Come on now.

She can't.

Oh, lie there.

She sits down. Mr Blake is in the doorway. She jumps.

You didn't knock.

Mr Blake The doors are always open in this street.

Mrs Shannon Well, you're not due today.

Mr Blake I know.

Mrs Shannon I can't pay.

Mr Blake Mrs Shannon, I had to be down here. I just popped in to tell you that I spoke to Mr Blakey.

Mrs Shannon And?

Mr Blake No go. He says he's put it to the solicitors. You must expect a summons.

Mrs Shannon I could pay you a pound.

Mr Blake Mrs Shannon, he's taken it out of the collector's hands. I just thought I'd tell you.

Mrs Shannon Doesn't he know from Mr Cottrell I'll pay?

Mr Blake Oh, you haven't heard about Mr Cottrell? Wasn't it terrible?

Mrs Shannon How would I hear? What?

Mr Blake He died, I'm afraid. Tuesday. Asphyxiated himself.

Mrs Shannon What himself?

Mr Blake Well, they operated, you know.

Mrs Shannon I knew that. I thought he was on the mend.

Mr Blake So we thought – but apparently they had found . . . Well you can guess.

Mrs Shannon And they told him?

Mr Blake Yes.

Mrs Shannon What did he do to himself?

Mr Blake His daughter brought him some fruit. In a polythene bag it was. He was in a side ward. He took the fruit out and ate it. I think they told him after that. He put the bag over his head.

She shudders.

Mrs Shannon And what then? What happens to you?

Mr Blake Well, he breathed it into him. Then of course that's it. You've had it. Suffocated him. Mrs Jones knew. I thought you all did down here.

She is shocked.

Mrs Shannon No.

Mr Blake Are you alright, Mrs Shannon?

Mrs Shannon Yes. Ha ha. (*She laughs.*) Whoops!

Mr Blake Steady.

Mrs Shannon Oh, I'm sorry.

Mr Blake I shouldn't have told you a thing like that. Do you feel sick?

Mrs Shannon No. No.

Mr Blake It does upset you, a thing like that.

Mrs Shannon I'm alright. (*Giggles.*) I'm not upset.

Mr Blake Well, I'd better be going. I only popped in,

Mrs Shannon I suppose you won't take the pound?

Mr Blake Well, I'm not meant to be here, Mrs Shannon, strictly speaking. Sorry. Don't see me out.

Mr Blake exits. She tries to wake her mother up.

Mrs Shannon Come on, Mama. Wake up now. (*She slaps her face. She lets her back into bed. She moves away. She smashes down a cup.*) Bang. Bang. (*violently*) What is it? What is it? Poor Mr Cottrell. What a thing to do. That's a terrible sin, that it is. (*She moves about, picking up the bits of crockery. She puts them on the table.*)

Pause.

What's allowing this? Things happen. You can't tell *me*. And the thing is, I know you can't. And it's no good me crowing. I'm not more of a woman than she is. Mama! She's a woman. She's been a woman. (*going to her*) Come on then, love. Come on, Mama. I'll make you some tea. Oh Mama, Mama. How could someone as cold as me feel that? And I can't.

She goes to the table and feels the surface with the palm of her hand. She examines the pieces of crockery. She sits down. Yawns. She gets into bed with her mother. Silence. Suddenly with no preparation she leaps up in the bed crying out. Then she gets up. She talks to herself but is hardly heard. Pause. Frankie enters.

Who's that?

Frankie Me. Who'd you expect? You got my tea? I got to go out.

Mrs Shannon Do you need clean socks? I got socks for you, clean.

Frankie Where?

Mrs Shannon Here. What do you want for tea?

Frankie Haven't you got anything?

Mrs Shannon What do you want? I can go and get something.

Frankie Well, you'd better. I'm going out.

Mrs Shannon I said I would. I'll go. Down the corner.

She exits. He sits down to unlace his boots. Looks at his mother for a long time. Flings a boot down wildly. Sits down. Long pause. Timid knock at the front door.

Frankie Yes.

Another knock

It's open. Mind the bike.

Mary Lynch knocks herself against the bike in the hall.

Mind yourself. Who is it?

Enter Mary Lynch.

Mary Mrs Shannon? Oh, I am sorry.

Frankie She's down the shop.

Mary I'm from the Legion of Mary.

Frankie I know. I met you.

Mary Oh yes. I said we might call again. If I wait, do you think she'll be long? Is she asleep?

Frankie Don't worry. Sit down.

Mary Oh. I will.

She sits. Frankie takes out the Echo.

Is your mother any better?

Frankie What? Oh, aye. Yes. She is. She is just the same.

Mary takes out a handkerchief. He puts the paper down.

Here, why didn't you knock louder?

Mary I beg your pardon?

Frankie Why did you knock like that?

Mary Like what?

Frankie Silly bloody knock.

Mary Was it?

Frankie I could have hit you silly.

Mary Oh. I'm sorry I'm sure. (*She puts her handkerchief to her nose.*)

Frankie What is the matter? Does it smell or something?

Mary No. Really, I've got a cold.

Frankie It smells though, doesn't it?

Mary Well a sick-room . . .

Frankie Yes. And we can't open the window. It's stuck.

Pause.

Mary I hate knocking. I dread it. I wait outside for hours sometimes. Daft, isn't it?

Frankie You want to learn to knock so people can hear you.

43

Mary Some people get very annoyed if you bang too hard.

Frankie You don't have to bang hard. Look, in case our Joan don't say anything. Just because we don't go to church much, don't keep coming round. Joan's got enough to do and I'm not always in, alright?

Mary And you're as good as those that go.

Frankie That's it.

Mary I never said you weren't.

His mother snores. He goes to her.

Frankie Wait a minute. She must be sleeping awkward. Snoring. Come on now.

Mary Shall I have you a hand?

Frankie Thanks.

Mary Should we sit her up, do you think?

Frankie Yes, I should think so.

Mary OK.

She tidies up the bed. He watches her. They sit.

Frankie Fag?

Mary Oh thanks.

Frankie What you doing down this way anyway?

Mary I have a friend that lives down here.

Frankie What you looking for? Ashtray. Here, use this.

Mary My mother was born over here.

Frankie Go on.

Mary Yes. North William Street.

Frankie Blimey. How old are you?

44

Mary Mind your own business.

Frankie This is all coming down, you know.

Mary Is it? When?

Frankie Well, we've had quittance. But they'll never do it.

Mary Have you indeed? Just as well, really, don't you think?

Frankie Indeed I don't. This is where we lives. Let them pull their own places down.

Mary If you go down the corner down here you can see where my Uncle Tommy wrote his name in the wet cement when they were first put up.

Frankie You wasn't born down here.

Mary No.

Frankie I didn't think you was. Our grandfathers came over here a hundred years ago and we still act as if there was a thing past we had to hammer out here. I was apprenticed to a trade. Lost my job. I goes on the docks. My father was born down here. We're superstitious. I don't know about anything else.

Old Mrs Shannon moans. They go to her.

Mary Is your mother alright? Have you ever worked away from here?

He negates with his head.

Haven't you? Not for National Service?

Frankie No. Unfit.

Mary Nor me. I got a job in Birmingham once. I could only stick it a fortnight. I can feel homesick without ever having been away from home. I feel foolish. As though someone had wrapped me up quickly in a rug to smother

45

the flames and then realised I hadn't been on fire in the first place.

Frankie I'm alright. What I'm afraid of is relying on the knowledge that everything could be alright. So I don't do anything about it. I'm afraid my hand will slip and I'll slice myself down in thick slices. Or I'll wake up and find terrible things I've done. Listen. What do you advise? You know my sister. You know my sister. I worked late last week. Nearly every night. She thought I didn't come home because I was out having a drink. I used to call in for a quick one, it was on my breath. She doesn't know how much I earned overtime. It is upstairs in my inside pocket some of it still. Nearly ten pounds it was and I haven't given her any extra this week either. What do you think?

Mary What?

Frankie What do you think?

Mary It's not my place to pass judgement, is it?

Frankie Yes, yes, but what's your opinion of what I should have done?

Mary Well, I don't know, do I?

Frankie Well, don't you think it's bad?

Mary I don't know. It's hardly anything to do with me.

Frankie Well, don't you think I should have gone to confession by now, at least?

Mary I should have thought there was something more practical you could do if you felt like it with ten pounds in your pocket.

Frankie It's not ten pounds now, anyway. What a thing to do, eh? She ought to go out more. My sister. Couldn't you tell her?

Mary Isn't she well?

Frankie She's not very fit. We're all a bit unfit. (*looking at his mother*) Her. She's just old.

Mary Oh really!

Frankie And she isn't either – fifty-eight, that's all she is. Remarkable isn't it? You ever been in hospital?

Mary Once, a gland. See?

Frankie Never noticed. It's alright, that.

Mary Yes.

Frankie Remember, do you?

Mary Vaguely.

Frankie I was in once through work. An operation. In a red-raw shape you are. Hot. Nurses enter. Say cool things. Little cows. I hate hospitals. Look at her, they had her in once.

Mary Your mother?

Frankie When she went funny first. She kept being sick. They opened her up to see what was what. And what did they find? Nothing. You wouldn't stay in your cot, would you? Kept trying to clamber out of your little bed with cot sides. Don't worry, she can't hear. There's nothing we can do. I'm going upstairs. You can stay if you want.

> *Frankie exits. She doesn't know what to do. She decides to leave the bag she's brought in the room. Mrs Shannon enters.*

Mary Hello, Mrs Shannon.

Mrs Shannon Oh, hello.

Mary You're not surprised to see me?

Mrs Shannon You said you might be back.

Mary Well, actually I'm not here for the Legion tonight.
I have other work this week. But I wanted to come down
off my own bat.

Mrs Shannon I've been down the shop. They've got a
dog down there.

Mary I've been talking to your brother.

Mrs Shannon Has he gone out?

Mary No. No. He's upstairs. I was going when you
came in. I was leaving this.

Mrs Shannon Oh yes.

Mary Well there are several things I never wear now.
Perfectly good. A coat – I thought of throwing them out,
but my mother thought it was a sin to do that. I know
there's always someone who could do with a perfectly
good coat. I hope you don't think it rude of me. Only it's
only to bring these I've come really. This week on my
Legion work I have to visit someone else. So this isn't
really on my work at all. They weren't old cast-offs, mind.
I wouldn't like you to think that. They weren't cheap when
they were new. There's some other things. A jumper
perhaps for Maria, If you don't think it's too old.

Mrs Shannon Oh, that's nice. Thanks.

Mary I hope the coat fits you. Don't try it on now.
That's all I came for really except to inquire after Mrs
Shannon.

Mrs Shannon I can't get her to wake this evening.

Mary The rest does her good, I'm sure. Well I must be
off. Oh, I forgot, I meant to give you this. We call it a
Tessara. It has the Legion prayers with a picture, you see?

Mrs Shannon Thanks.

Mary I must be going.

Mrs Shannon Must you? Well, thank you and that.

Mary Don't mention it. I hope you didn't mind?

Mrs Shannon No.

Mary Perhaps I'll see you anyway. One day perhaps outside church.

Mrs Shannon Yes. I expect so.

Mary Goodnight, then. Is it dark out?

Pause.

Mrs Shannon Yes, it's getting quite dark.

They exit. Pause. Mrs Shannon re-enters.

Frankie?

Frankie (*off*) What?

Mrs Shannon Do you want this tea?

Frankie No. It's alright.

Mrs Shannon But I got it.

Frankie Well, keep it. I don't want it.

She goes into the kitchen. He comes down.

Mrs Shannon You going out?

Frankie Yes.

Mrs Shannon What time will you be back? Usual?

Frankie Where's the shoe polish?

Mrs Shannon I don't know if we've got any. Look in the cupboard. What time are you in in the morning? Same?

He finds an empty tin.

Frankie Yes. Leave the clock.

Mrs Shannon OK.

He goes. Door slams. She comes back into the room.

Maria. Our Maria. You're not in. Our Frankie. Frankie.
Not in. Our Mama. Wake up now, Mama. Come on,
Mama. Wake up. Wake up. (*desperate*) Get up. Get up.
Wake up. Our Frankie! Our Lord have mercy on us.
Jesus, Mary and Joseph. I'm scalded. (*She goes to the
bag and takes out the clothes to inspect them.*) Let's have
a look, then. What's Father Christmas brought us?
That'll do Maria. (*She takes out the coat.*) What about
this? (*She tries it on.*) I don't like red. It doesn't fit. (*She
takes it off and drops it on the floor.*) Ah, what's the use
of strangers? Why did I leave this table? (*She pushes
away the things on it.*) My ankles are cold. (*She sits
down and rubs her ankles.*) I ought to stop. I ought to
stop it. (*She gets up and bangs on the wall.*) Mrs Hayes!
(*Bangs.*) Mrs Hayes! (*Bangs – no reply.*) Look at this
place. (*She examines the club book and the Legion
leaflet Mary gave her.*) I'll give this place a good tidy
tomorrow. It's a bit late to start anything now. (*Absently
she tears the leaflet and book over the coat on the floor.*)
I'll see if I can't change that bed and all. I did that. Then.
Ours is a nice house, ours is.

*She pulls the table towards the door. She pushes the
sideboard against the door. She pushes the table
against the sideboard.*

At this time. At this moment, am I? (*Her head rolls back,
eyes and mouth open.*) Get up, Mama! Come on, time to
get up. Now. This minute! Oh! it's terrible. Oh, this is
quite terrible.

She sits down. Pause.

Now I don't feel that. Now I feel – (*Pause.*) How much
dirt on my skin? How much dirt in my hair? How many
hairs on my head? I see things look at me calmly as I am
looking at them or see things living as I am living. At
this precise second which has passed. At these precise
seconds which are passing. (*Pause.*) I could leave. I could
go. I could say. If I could get rid of this at the back of
my head. That it doesn't matter. Nibbling at the top of
my neck like a mouse under here. (*She imitates the little
squeals of a mouse.*) And our Frankie's so full of himself.
So full. Of himself. What does he do with himself? (*She
gets up.*) But I feel I am coming to it. That one day it'll
happen.

> She touches things in the room. She asks herself a
> question.

Do you? (*The reply is torn involuntarily.*) Yes! Yes!

> She is agitated. She quietens down.

Oh dear. Isn't it awful? It's quite awful. Mama, damn it,
how many more times do I have to call you? I should
have asked that Legion woman for a lend. Oh dear, dear,
dear.

> She sits. She leans forward as if with a stomach ache.
> Rocks herself backwards and forwards. She hums two
> notes monotonously in rhythm. She stops. Sighs. She
> whistles a tune. Silence.
> She crawls into bed with her mother.
> End of Act Two.

Act Three

The next day.
  Mrs Shannon is sitting up in bed drinking a cup of tea.
Old Mrs Shannon is in the armchair.

Mrs Shannon You don't know what you're missing. You
should have had a cup, when I said. The pot's empty
now and you're not having any of mine either. (*Drinks.*)
Lovely. I can do with this. I really can. I think I deserve
a cup. You don't know what you're missing. (*Pause.*)
I haven't half got a headache. And not an aspirin can
I find. I shall have to recourse to vinegar and brown
paper. There's an old remedy you'll remember. Many's
the time I've seen you with curtains drawn and a dish
of vinegar there and brown paper tied round your head
with a stocking, over the other house. (*She finishes the
tea.*) Lovely grub. Lovely. You should have had a cup,
I'd have another but I don't think I deserve two. (*Pause.*)
I think I'll get up in a minute. You. You can look. And
what did you do? Apart from what you tried to do.
Attempted to do. Go on then. Go and lie down if you
want to. I don't care. I think you're silly. You ought to
fight it. But go and lie down if you want to. I'm going
out. I should have gone out. You. What do you look
like, eh? Smart-looking, aren't you? Go on. Go on then.
(*She hides under the clothes. She comes out again.*) Oh
Christ, what a bloody day. I'm getting up. (*Pause.*) Here
I am sitting and she's over there and that's us. I'm getting
littler with all the things I'm doing till I'll dwindle to a
little rat. Bright eyes. Small human parts. I've such a
small figure, just like her. (*feeling her breasts*) Fine list

of things I do, I must say. What does that add me up to?
Half-eaten bits and pieces around the place. Oh nothing.
Look at what kind of washing-up I do. What do you
expect me to do? Hop on to my back and I'll sing to
you. (*She leans back and picks up the cup.*) Any more.
No. In a train once I afforded the tea. I expect it was
then. I know there was this particular time. I was on
a train. Now where was it? That time. Do you know,
I can't for the life of me place it. Anyway. I had tea on
a train once. Exorbitant prices for what they give you,
and the tea! It could hardly make its way out of the
pot. Must have cost about twopence a quarter. Anyway.
What was I saying? (*She lies back.*)

Maria speaks through the door.

Maria Mama.

Mrs Shannon Yes.

Maria It's Maria.

Mrs Shannon Is it now?

Maria Mama.

Mrs Shannon What?

Maria I've come in.

Mrs Shannon What do you expect me to do about it?

Maria Can't I come in?

Mrs Shannon Does it look like it?

Maria I want a drink of water.

Mrs Shannon Go next door for a drink of water.

Maria What would they say?

Mrs Shannon How do I know what they'll say?

Maria Mama.

Mrs Shannon Go down Christine's,

Maria I stayed down there last night.

Mrs Shannon Go again.

Maria What about dinner?

Mrs Shannon I haven't got any.

Maria It's dinner time.

Mrs Shannon I'm bad in bed.

Maria You are not.

Mrs Shannon I'm bad.

Maria You are not.

Mrs Shannon I'm in bed.

Maria Mama.

Mrs Shannon Go on.

Maria Mama.

Mrs Shannon Go on, I said.

Maria goes. Mrs Shannon leans back.

Oh yes. Definitely. Oh!

*She is lying down. She hits the side of the cup with
a spoon. She puts her arms in the air. Looks at her
hand.*

I'm happy. O Jesus. I'm happy.

Maria knocks.

Maria Mama. (*Pause.*) Mama.

Mrs Shannon Go on, I said.

Maria Are you bad, Mama?

Mrs Shannon I'm alright. Go on.

Maria Can I see you're alright?

Mrs Shannon Go on when you're told.

Maria I'm not going.

Mrs Shannon Well, sit out there then.

Maria Mama.

Knock.

Mama.

Mrs Shannon What?

Maria You know, Mama.

Mrs Shannon I don't know.

Maria You know, Mama.

Mrs Shannon I know you.

Maria Don't act daft, Mama. Mama. Come on, Mama, be good now.

Mrs Shannon Shut up, will you, and go out and play.

Maria I don't want to play.

Mrs Shannon Well, stick out there then.

Maria I'll tell.

Mrs Shannon You tell who you like.

Maria Don't worry, I will.

Mrs Shannon Good.

Maria I'll come in.

Mrs Shannon Alright, come in then.

Maria I'm coming in.

Mrs Shannon Go on then.

Maria I will.

Mrs Shannon Come on then. Go on then, push then, why don't you? You will, will you? Will you? Eh? I know you. I knew you wouldn't. Maria? Are you still there? Maria. Maria. Oh! (*Long pause.*) I should take this cup out, shouldn't I? You should have had some tea. You're lazy, you are. Oh you're so lazy. You are, you are. What about that? What about that, eh? What about denying it happened. *It* happened. What about that time I was going on the boat and you made me fall in and I had to come home? Go on, get out. What about that pear you gave me and the caterpillar crawling out as I bit it. *You* gave that to me. You can remember. Yes you can. You can remember giving it. (*She feels her breasts.*) What do you think you're doing dressed up like that, eh? What have you got on, eh? I won't stop. Get out of it.

> *She cringes. She puts her hands over the left side of her face as if trying to get far away from something behind her left-hand side.*

Go on. Go on. Oh. (*as if she's got something in front of her*) Why do you have to giggle like that? Oh Mama. You don't know what you're laughing at half the time. It was a simple enough thing he said. It's no good going into explanations. It's not even a joke. What are you giggling for? There's nothing not to understand. It's nothing. He made a remark. Don't just giggle. There's nothing to be afraid of. You're alright. What you laughing for? Stop laughing. They're laughing at you. Don't belittle yourself. Don't join in with them. It started over nothing. Don't laugh. Come on. Come to me. Come

on, lovey, to me. It's alright. Stop it. Stop it. Let them just
think on. You silly fool. You silly. Don't come giggling
round here. I don't want you. Shoo. Go on. Go on.
Go on. (*She's kneeling up in bed.*) I seen you. I seen you.
What were you doing? What were you all covered in?
And your head. A tin of . . . with a tin key. I could
have. I could have. What am I eating? I could. I could.
(*violently with flailing arms*) Get up off the floor. Oh
come on. Get up. Get. Please, up.

> *Eventually she is lying face down. Pause. Frankie*
> *bangs hard on the door.*

What's that?

Frankie It's Frank.

Mrs Shannon You're not there.

Frankie I am here.

Mrs Shannon You're not.

Frankie We are.

Mrs Shannon You're not.

Frankie We are, love.

Mrs Shannon You can't come in.

Frankie What makes you think I want to?

Mrs Shannon Where's Maria?

Frankie A lot you care.

Mrs Shannon Alright, keep her. Keep her!

> *Long pause.*

Frankie Come on now, Joan. I've had enough of this.
Joan, I'll have to come in sometime.

Mrs Shannon Will you?

Frankie Yes.

Mrs Shannon Will you now?

Frankie What about the food, for example?

Mrs Shannon Don't worry about that.

Frankie But, Joan, if we can't get in, I'll have to worry.

Mrs Shannon No. Don't bother.

Frankie What do you mean, don't bother?

Mrs Shannon What I say. Don't bother.

Frankie But I'll have to bother.

Mrs Shannon Look, get out, will you.

Frankie What do you mean get out. I want to get in.

Mrs Shannon Well, you can't.

Frankie But this is the house.

Mrs Shannon There's other rooms.

Frankie Well.

Mrs Shannon Well.

Frankie I've got to come in. There's things to see to.

Mrs Shannon That's hard lines.

Frankie I'm coming in.

Mrs Shannon You'd better not.

Frankie I think I better had.

Mrs Shannon I shouldn't if I was you.

Frankie I could if I wanted to.

Mrs Shannon You couldn't.

Frankie Want me to try it then?

Mrs Shannon Don't come in! Don't come in!

Long pause.

Frankie You know what your trouble is, don't you, Joan? You don't eat enough.

Mrs Shannon (*quietly, to her mother*) Mama! Mama!

Frankie Isn't that right? You never sit down to a proper meal, do you? Joan!

Mrs Shannon What?

Pause.

Frankie I'm going now.

Mrs Shannon I've heard that before.

Frankie Well, I can't walk out of work just when I feel like it.

Mrs Shannon Who's keeping you?

Frankie I'll be back later. (*Pause.*) Joan!

Mrs Shannon Will you? (*Pause.*) Have you gone, Frankie?

Frankie No.

Mrs Shannon They'll give you the push if you don't watch it. (*Pause.*) Are you going? (*Pause.*) Frankie.

Frankie Yes. (*Pause.*) Yes. (*Pause.*) I'm sick of you. I'm sick of you. You.

Mrs Shannon Haven't you been to work?

Frankie No.

Mrs Shannon Don't be silly, Frankie. Go back to work.

Frankie I'm not going back to work.

Mrs Shannon Don't be silly, Frankie.

Frankie Oh shut up, can't you. Just keep that quiet.
(*Pause.*) I am going back to work. Right? I am going
back to work. You want to watch it, that's all.

Silence.

Frankie I wish she'd . . . I wish she'd . . .

Mrs Shannon (*overlapping*) Exorbitant prices. The prices.

He weeps.

Now don't start crying, Frankie. You big soft thing. Now
go away. Now stop it.

Pause.

Frankie I'm going now.

Pause. He bangs the door.

Joan.

Pause. Front door slam. Pause.

Mrs Shannon He, Frankie. Are you there? Francis.
You . . . You're out there, aren't you? Frankie. Frankie.
Francis.

*She's out of bed. She tries to pull the chest away from
the door but doesn't succeed.*

Our Blessed Lady I'm going to die of this. Run about
in here. Smells and faces I don't want before me again.
I can smell your powder in my nose, Mama. And them
banks in a rockery above the seaside. When I was ill,
you had a yellow face. You were mean to me. You
weren't. Oh. Oh. Frankie. (*Pause.*) Look, I'll get a flannel
to wash both our faces.

She goes into the kitchen. Pause. Comes back with a flannel.

Here we are.

She looks at her mother. She wipes her own face. Without looking in that direction she flings the flannel away.

I did that. And things that happened. Faces I had of you aren't you. They're only pictures of someone like you. Look at you. I don't know you.

Suddenly she takes a knife which she has been concealing and makes to drive it into her mother. She drops it.

There. Come on. Up we get. Come on. I'll carry you.

With effort she takes her mother into the kitchen.

Come on. Out we go. Come on.

Pause. She comes back in and closes the door. Pause. She gathers all the bedclothes and pulls them off the bed, leaving the mattress bare.
The End.

OVER GARDENS OUT

Over Gardens Out was first performed in the Theatre Upstairs at the Royal Court Theatre on 5 August 1968 with the following cast:

Mrs B Pamela Miles
Jeffry Don Hawkins
Dennis James Hazeldine
Mother June Watson
Father Anthony Douse
Shop Assistant Roger Nott

Directed by Peter Gill

Characters

Mrs B

Jeffry

Dennis

Mother

Father

Shop Assistant

Jeffry is a Londoner

Note

When *Over Gardens Out* was performed in the
Theatre Upstairs at the Royal Court Theatre
two television sets were placed one each side of the
playing area, against the theatre walls. They were
each tuned to a different station and the volumes
remote-controlled so that during the play the sound
could be turned down except in scenes where a
television might be on. The sound was brought up
at the end of some of the scenes to help cover
the stage management moving the furniture,
and both sets were turned up when the audience
came in and when they left the theatre.

SCENE ONE

Jeffry is eating his tea. Mrs B. is standing near him. The baby is in his pram. Pause.

Mrs B Alright?

Jeffry nods. Pause.

I'll fill it up.

She goes to the baby's pram and picks a toy up off the floor. She goes into the kitchen. She brings the kettle in. Fills the teapot. Exits with the kettle and Jeffry's plate. Jeffry pours himself a cup of tea. Gets up.

Jeffry Do you want one? (*He pours her a cup. Walks about, cup in hand. Looks into the pram.*) I think his nose is bleeding. Ay. You'd better come here. His nose is bleeding. Ay.

Mrs B (*enters*) What! Jesus! O my God! (*Goes to the baby.*) Jeffry, you silly sod. I nearly died of fright. He's all right. It's just his nose running. What did you say that for? He's just got a cold. Mind. (*She gets a handkerchief.*) What do you want to say a thing like that for?

Jeffry I thought it was red. Sorry. (*to the baby*) Sorry, mate.

Mrs B There. (*She sits to drink her tea. Pause.*)

Jeffry Can I iron my shirt?

Mrs B I'll do it.

Jeffry No, I'll do it.

69

Mrs B I'm going ironing now, in a minute.

Jeffry I'll do it.

Mrs B The iron's on.

He begins to iron.

Jeffry Where's Harry?

Mrs B Working late, I suppose.

Jeffry Again?

Mrs B He's working all the hours God made lately.

Jeffry He must be stacking it away.

Mrs B He doesn't tell me if he does then. Is that too dry?

Jeffry No, it's alright. Doesn't matter. Has he been good today?

Mrs B Who?

Jeffry (*indicates the baby*) Him.

Mrs B Oh yeah. He's no bother. Are you? He's as good as gold.

Jeffry (*to the baby*) Are you?

Mrs B I'd better wash up and put his back on. He shouldn't be long.

Jeffry There we are. Do you want any of this done?

Mrs B No, there's only some of the baby's things I was going to do. I'll wait till the morning. I can't be bothered.

Jeffry No it's easy. Here watch this.

She exits.
  Jeffry talks to the baby as he works.

This is yours. Look at that for ironing, boy. (*He shows the baby the finished ironing.*) Look at that, Rog. You won't find a better piece of work than that, I can tell you. What did you say? Yes, I know. You're the best thing since sliced bread.

Mrs B (*off*) Are you going out, Jeffry?

Jeffry I might. Why?

Mrs B No reason.

Jeffry (*picking up a man's shirt*) I shan't do his shirt. You know how fussy he is about his collars.

Mrs B Right you are.

Jeffrey picks up napkin.

Jeffry This don't need ironing, do it?

Mrs B What?

Jeffry This just needs airing, dun it?

Mrs B I'll do them, Jeffry.

Jeffry (*to himself*) I might as well put the iron over it. See that, my son? See what I do for you? I don't do this for everybody, you know.

Mrs B What say?

Jeffry (*to the baby*) Did you like that? (*He goes over to the baby. Looks alarmed.*) Hey!

Mrs B What. What?

Jeffry (*shaking the baby*) Ah, it's alright. (*to the baby*) Christ, you don't half lie still sometimes, you do.

SCENE TWO

Dennis is sitting in an armchair. His father is polishing his shoes, one foot on a chair. His mother is getting ready to go out.

Dennis This is a change, you two going out. Where are you going?

Mother Down the club. You know, we told you.

Dennis Put out the flags.

Mother We've no need of your sarcasm, thank you. (*She powders her nose in the oval mirror on the wall.*)

Dennis The room looks very dusty in this light.

She puts lipstick on, using her little finger.

I want to come. Just because I don't ever make a fuss.

Mother You could have come.

Dennis You didn't ask me.

Father Here. Here. Don't let's have an upset, son.

Dennis Oh, you're with us, are you?

Mother You could have come. (*She puts her make-up in her bag.*)

Dennis I don't want to come.

Father Well, what did you say you did for?

Mother He's always the same. He just tries it on to make things awkward.

Dennis No, I don't.

Mother Alright then. We'll stay in. (*She puts on a short coat.*)

Dennis I don't want you to stay in. I know that coat. What are you trying to do?

Mother Nothing.

Dennis What are you wearing that coat for then?

Mother I'll need a coat later.

Dennis Take it off. Put it back.

Father Come on, leave him. (*Exits.*)

Mother (*she adjusts her stockings*) You're a little cat, you are.

Dennis I'm not a little cat. Go out if you want to.

Mother Well, God knows, Dennis, you're old enough to be left alone.

Dennis I want to be. Go on.

Mother Haven't you got anything to do?

Dennis No.

Father (*off*) Come on, Mother.

Mother Well, that's hardly my fault, is it?

Dennis I didn't say it was.

Mother (*puts on her gloves*) What's wrong with this coat?

Dennis You should see yourself.

Mother It's alright.

Dennis That's what you think.

She sits down.

Well, go on, if you're going. (*Pause.*) Now don't be like that. I haven't done anything. Go on.

Mother I'm not going.

Dennis Go on. Go on.

Mother No, I don't think I want to, thank you.

Father (*off*) Are you coming?

Mother No. You go on without me.

Father (*coming in*) What?

Mother I'm not going.

Father Don't be silly.

Mother I'm not being silly. I'm just not going.

Father Now look, are you coming or aren't you?

Mother No.

Father Come on.

Mother No, I said.

Dennis Make her go.

Father Come on. (*Pause.*) You want to get some sense, Dennis, you do. (*Pause.*) Well, I'm going anyway. I'll stroll on. I'll wait for you down the end. (*Pause.*) Alright? (*Pause. Exits.*)

Dennis Don't stay in just because of me.

   Door slams.

Mother You always take the pleasure out of everything, you do. Somehow.

Dennis That's right. Blame me. (*Pause.*) Aren't you going? Eh? I'll be alright. Go on, Mum. Will you? Oh, go on. Will you? (*He lowers his head in despair.*)

Mother (*she rises*) Don't you be up late. Do you hear me? Dennis?

74

Dennis Alright.

Mother I don't know what time we'll be back.

Dennis OK.

Mother There's a banana out there for you.

Dennis Smashing.

Mother Well, see if there's anything else you want.
You're a contrary bloody kid. Goodnight, God bless.

Dennis Have a good time.

She exits.

SCENE THREE

Dennis and Jeffry enter with a large sheet.

Jeffry We'll get nicked.

Dennis What do you want this for?

Jeffry Watch it. Watch I don't get you.

Dennis What do you want this for? We'll get nicked.
That was that woman's washing. What do you want it
for? We don't want it.

Jeffry Hold it. Hold it. (*He rips through the sheet with
a knife.*) Ha, ha, ha. We'll get nicked. (*He whistles like a
bird.*)

Dennis What are you going to do with it?

Jeffry You can have it.

Dennis I don't want it. You'd better hide it.

Jeffry How if I wrapped barbed wire round my fists?
Of course, I'd have to have a glove on and then . . . Or.

If you put your thumbs there. (*He puts his thumbs into Dennis's eyes.*) Out they'd pop. (*He spars, playing.*) I could eat you between two bits of bread. You know. You could put people on the ground. I mean put their bare feet over a bamboo shoot and then in no time it shoots up and finds a foot in the way, but it can't stop so it grows through it. You know they bend saplings? You know that. I should like to have someone in the corner of a room all bandages. They'd be in a mess after punishment. Or make you swallow a mouse. I'd like to tie someone up. Punish them. Belt fuck out of them and then tape it. Put it on tape. Then I'd tie them up and play it back. And then start over again.

Pause.

Let's go over the park.

Dennis It'll be closed.

Jeffry Not yet.

Dennis He'll be closing.

Jeffry We can get out.

Dennis How?

Jeffry Climb over.

Dennis You ever see me climb?

Jeffry Well, squeeze through then. You're skinny enough. Let's go over the allotments then.

Dennis What for?

Jeffry Pick the beans. Lush they are about now. Get in among the bean poles.

Dennis What are we going to do with this?

Jeffry That's your lookout.

Dennis It isn't.

Jeffry You nicked it.

Dennis I never did.

Jeffry Well, I don't care what you do with it.

They hear an ice-cream van. Some famous tune played electronically.

Do you fancy an ice-cream?

Dennis I don't mind. What van is it?

Jeffry Eyetalian. The Walls' one comes early. He comes late.

Dennis I'd rather Walls'.

Jeffry Fucking choosey, ain't you? Our baby'd rather the early one and all.

Dennis Your baby?

Jeffry He generally has a taste of one this weather. How much are they?

Dennis I'll pay.

Jeffry No. I'll pay.

Dennis No. Let me pay, let me pay. I want to pay.

Jeffry Alright. You're like a little child, aren't you?

Dennis I'm older than you.

Jeffry You want to act it then.

Ice-cream van heard again.

You're a bit late anyway, there goes the van.

Dennis Come on, then. We'll catch it up.

Jeffry No. Leave it.

Dennis Come on. I'll get there first.

Jeffry Will you?

They run off

SCENE FOUR

Dennis and Jeffry enter eating ice-creams.

Dennis You shouldn't have left that behind.

Jeffry What?

Dennis That thing.

Jeffry What thing?

Dennis That thing off the line.

Jeffry Where'd you put it?

Dennis In a hedge.

Jeffry That was a nice thing to do, wasn't it?

Dennis Well I had to do something.

Jeffry Let's go over the park. On the swings.

Dennis No. I don't want to. (*Pause.*)

Jeffry You ever been to camp?

Dennis Of course.

Jeffry What d'you mean, of course? Who'd you go with, the scouts?

Dennis No. Who'd you go with?

Jeffry The school.

Dennis Oh, ay.

Jeffry Did they pull your trousers down?

78

Dennis Where?

Jeffry Camping. Did they? I bet they pulled your trousers down.

Dennis No, they didn't. Why should they? Yes, they did.

Jeffry pulls out a magazine.

Jeffry Here, have a look at her.

Dennis What is it?

Jeffry *Parade*. I collect it. Do you get it?

Dennis Never seen it.

Jeffry You don't know what you're missing. (*to the magazine*) Cop hold of this darling. You can have it. I got that one already.

Dennis I don't want it.

Jeffry Give it back then. Look at her. That one's a reject. I collect them.

Dennis Since when?

Jeffry Since last year, clever. I'm on the track of four. There's four I'm on the track of and then I'm up to date. There's a bit about Karate in this one. I was reading there's only two Karate experts in the world. I wouldn't like to meet either of them. One of them defeated forty of the Japanese Imperial Guard single-handed. There's five weak spots in the human body. The human body is a very tough machine. You see in films or you read about how someone gets stabbed – so easy – and the blood and then they're dead. Well, let me tell you, you get a bowie and bang it into someone's gut hard, and it still only goes in two and a half inches. You won't kill the human animal that easy. There are five weak spots in the human body. Here – the sleeping spot, the axis. Just behind the ears – very sensitive spot. Here. And the solar plexus.

Dennis Where else?

Jeffry Where do you think? People think it's all hand work, too.

Dennis Do they?

Jeffry See that edge. Chop. That's not the half of it. There's all the foot work. The holds. I haven't done any of that. I don't think I will either. You've got to have all this edge and the fingers. Like bone. The same with the feet. It could get dangerous. You've had it if you do Karate properly – with the law. Really you should register yourself as an offensive weapon.

Dennis You'd think they'd make it illegal.

Jeffry Don't talk soft. It's an ancient sport, isn't it?

Dennis Like Judo.

Jeffry It isn't like Judo at all. What do you say that for? It is not like Judo one bit. Shows how much you know. Judo is bloody useless. Judo's a defence sport. Karate's attacking. There's all the difference in the world, isn't there?

Dennis Well, how was I to know? (*Pause.*)

Jeffry You ever take any?

Dennis What?

Jeffry Hearts or poppers. I used to use old inhalers. I gave it up.

Dennis No, I haven't.

Jeffry You want to try. It's extraordinary.

Dennis Is it?

Jeffry Yes. With amphetamines, it makes you want to wash all the time.

Dennis What?

Jeffry I can't keep out of the bathroom. I keep shaving. I have to go to the window all the time. You could knock me down wiv a fevver If I'm stoned. I ain't had none since I been down here. Don't seem no point. When you get stoned you can't get a hard on. Then you can't get it off. Or it shrinks. You know that. Till it's hardly bloody there. It's bloody funny. You can't hardly see it. Like a winkle.

Dennis Really?

Jeffry Honest. (*Pause.*) I read in that, it's against some religions to kill even insects. Even insects you couldn't see.

Dennis Yes. In those places they think that if they take it that far somehow the misery most of the actual people lives in won't seem so bad.

Jeffry Are you religious?

Dennis Not very.

Jeffry I'm not.

Dennis Have you had your tea?

Jeffry Course I have, had it straight after work. Ain't you had none?

Dennis I come straight out. I'm starving.

Jeffry You just had an ice-cream.

Dennis I never said I didn't. How much do you pay in your digs?

Jeffry Three pound ten all in.

Dennis Not bad.

Jeffry I never said it was.

Dennis Do you want some chips?

Jeffry What, after ice-cream?

Dennis I haven't had no tea.

Jeffry That's your look-out.

Dennis Come on, let's go down Carlisle, we can have some on the way back.

Jeffry I'm not having the Greeks.

Dennis I never said you was, did I?

Jeffry Just so we get it straight. Bloody greasy hole. You're a proper little guts, ain't yer? Eh, gutsy, aren't yer? Gutsy, aren't yer? Ain't yer?

They exit.

SCENE FIVE

Dennis and Jeffry.

Jeffry We had some laughs In that school, mind. I'll say we did. Especially after we'd done something wrong. They weren't meant to hit us, you know, really, but we got our fair share. If someone in our room had done something wrong. Like there was this woman once looking at us when we were waiting in a line in the town. You could tell where we was from. Anyway, she was looking at us, and Ray, that was my mate, he went and gobbed right at her. Like that. And told her to fuck off. We weren't half in for it. I used to keep an eye open for Ray. He was only the size of twopence. He had an

auntie once come to see him. We got split up when I got
put on remand. After I bolted that was. There was this
old tart, the matron she was, and she used to have to
supervise our bath. Well, I reckon she was looking at me
a bit old-fashioned one night so I stared back at her.
'What are you looking at?' she says. 'What are you
looking at?' I says. 'What are you looking at?' she says.
My arse and the shit up my arse, I grabbed it and hit her.
I hit the superintendent too. They didn't do nothing to
me. I scarpered. They got me, though. He used to grin,
Ray, like you do.

Dennis I don't grin.

Jeffry You do grin.

Dennis Don't say I grin.

Jeffry Won't I?

Dennis When people say you grin, they despise you. If
someone grins they're inferior to you. Also they hate you.

Jeffry You going in?

Dennis Oh, not yet.

Jeffry I am.

Dennis Oh, don't go in yet.

Jeffry Why not?

Dennis Stay out a bit longer.

Jeffry No. I'm going in. Might as well.

Dennis Don't go in yet.

Jeffry Why not? What for?

Dennis Come on, let's go over the park.

Jeffry No, I'm going in.

Dennis Tara then.

Jeffry Tara.

SCENE SIX

Dennis sitting indoors. Father is gardening.

Mother (*off*) Have you gone out, Dennis? Dennis!

Dennis What?

Mother (*entering*) You were very quiet. Where's your father?

Dennis How should I know.

Mother He was in the garden.

Dennis In the what?

Mother He was getting in some potatoes.

Dennis Shall we have some?

Mother For your supper? If you like.

Dennis That won't be bad. He has his uses.

Mother He's still out there. Dennis, what do you have to tell lies for?

Dennis I never noticed him. (*Mother goes out to Father.*)

Mother If you're going to church, Arthur, you'll have to step on it. (*She gets some washing in.*) What do you think of that, dry as a bone. I only put them out this afternoon.

Father Perfect weather. (*Pause.*) I say, perfect weather.

Mother Lovely.

Father There we are. How will that do? (*Shows her bowl of potatoes.*)

Mother Perfect. I'll do some for when you get back.

Father I might go for a pint after.

Mother Oh, aye.

Father I'll just have the one. (*He comes in to wash his hands.*)

Mother (*calling over to another garden*) Weather dry enough for you? Lovely, isn't it? Has he had his holidays? No. Nor Arthur. (*She goes in whistling.*)

   Father comes in to put his shoes on.

Father It's a lovely evening out, son.

   Mother comes in.

Mother Dry as a bone. (*Puts clothes down.*)

Father You going out, son? (*Pause.*) What's up with him?

Mother No good asking me. As if I'd know.

Dennis Where are you going?

Father I'm going to church.

Dennis Good for you.

Father That's where you'd be going if you had any sense.

Dennis Like you, you mean.

Father You want to give less lip.

Mother No, now, now. Look at that cat, Dennis. Aren't they neat? See where your father's just been digging. Now you watch. You see? It will make a little place.

There. Now . . . See? Now it will bury it. See its paws.
I don't like them. But they're marvellous animals for
keeping clean.

Father Right, Mother, pass me my muffler. I don't need
a shave.

Dennis You can't go out like that. You'll have to wear a
tie. Tell him.

Father Alright then. Pass me the tie. Anything for a bit
of peace.

Mother You've got such standards, Dennis. I wonder if
you'll ever live up to them yourself.

Father Where's my clips? I think I'll take the bike.

Dennis What, that old wreck? You can't ride that.

Mother Be quiet. You used to be such a nice boy,
Dennis.

Dennis I believe you adopted me anyway.

Mother Oh, Dennis, don't be such a child.

Dennis Why haven't you got any more children then?
Bloody funny, if you ask me. I bet the papers are upstairs
in that bag. I shall have a look one day when you're out,
so I shall know.

Mother You dare. That's all. You just dare look into my
private property.

Father Now then. Now then. My word, you're a nasty
kid at times. I'm going then. Tara. (*He goes.*)

Dennis sits. Mother folds the washing.

Mother (*finishes*) That'll do.

*Dennis puts on the wireless. Finds some music. Begins
to dance. Stops. Switches it off.*

86

Dennis Shall I do your hair for you?

Mother Not now, I'm just having a quiet fag. Get on with your dancing.

Dennis Can I have one?

Mother No, I'd watch it. I'm not wasting a cigarette on you.

Dennis Go on.

Mother Now, no.

Dennis Mam.

Mother Now shut up, Dennis. You'll only choke yourself to death and be sick.

Dennis I won't.

Mother You'll get cancer.

Dennis You've got to die some way.

Mother Christ give me patience!

Dennis Go on, give us a fag.

Mother You've got me scalded.

Dennis Well give me a puff of yours.

Mother Honest to God, isn't it terrible? I sat down for a little bit of peace.

Dennis Just a drag.

Mother You'll wet the end.

Dennis I won't.

Mother Shit, shut up. No.

Dennis (*giggles*) Don't swear.

Mother If I go to hell it'll be your doing. Now sit down and read, there's a good boy. (*Pause.*)

Dennis Mam.

Mother I've gone out.

Dennis Give us a puff.

Mother I'll give you a punch. You soft get.

Dennis (*giggles*) Don't swear.

Mother Now don't start giggling, Dennis. I don't think I could stand it.

He giggles.

Shut up, you silly soft mare.

He giggles.

Honest, I think there's something wrong with you. It's a terrible thing to say about your own child, I know.

Dennis Give us a drag. A little drag.

Mother Here. Here. I hope it chokes you.

He takes it.

Look at you. You're like the chimp in the advert.

Dennis I don't know what you see in them.

Mother They're the only bit of pleasure I *do* get. Now, give it back to me. Dennis, what have you done to the end? It is all wet. Here, put it out for me.

He does so.

Dennis Let's comb your hair.

Mother Alright. But no pulling mind, d'you hear me?

Mother sits and dozes. Dennis does her hair but gives up. He wanders about. He sits. Plays with his mother's

handbag. Fiddles with the radio, changing the stations.
He takes his mother's mirror out of her bag. Puts her
spectacles on. Puts her lipstick on.

Mother What you doing?

Dennis Nothing.

Mother I don't like the sound of that.

Dennis I'm not. (*Giggles.*) Look. (*Shows her.*)

Mother Take them off, Dennis. Go on. You'll break
them.

Dennis I won't. I'm only playing.

Mother You just break them, that's all. (*Pause.*) What's
that noise, Dennis?

Dennis It's a bluebottle, I think.

Mother Where?

Dennis In the window, trying to get out.

Mother Kill it, Dennis, there's a good boy. Nasty thing.

Dennis Come here. Come here. (*Kills it under curtain.*)
Want the body?

Mother Ugh! Don't be disgusting.

Dennis walks up and down singing 'Stormy Weather'
incessantly.

Dennis
'Can't go on, everything I do is wrong.
Stormy weather . . .'

Mother Dennis, stop walking up and down, will you,
you're driving me mad. Haven't you got a nice book to
read? (*Pause. She dozes.*)

Dennis No. (*Pushes her.*) Come on, wake up. Don't go to sleep. Mam!

Mother (*smacking him*) Don't be so spiteful, Dennis.

Dennis Mam. (*Tries to get on her lap.*)

Mother Get off, you great lump. You're too heavy. Come on then.

> *She takes him on her lap, arms round him. Quiet. He suddenly gets up and moves quickly across the room.*

Can't you keep quiet for five minutes, Dennis?

Dennis I'm going out. Tara.

Mother Don't you be late, do you hear me?

SCENE SEVEN

Dennis and Jeffry enter.

Dennis You're a bit of a fool, aren't you? (*Giggles.*)

Jeffry Right. You've had it now. You've got it coming to you later. That's one punishment for a start. Any more offences to be taken into account? Eh? Eh?

Dennis Seriously though, you're a bit of an idiot, aren't you? (*Giggles.*)

Jeffry What? Do you want it now? Yes. Yes. Yes. Do you? Do you want it? Do you want it? Tell me.

Dennis Yes. No. Yes. Ow! Leggo. Aye, you hurt me, you did. (*Giggles.*) Really though, you are a bit thick. Fair do's.

Jeffry Right. That's a beating later. Don't worry, missis, he'll lick my shoes later.

Dennis There's no one to hear you. What are you going to make me do?

Jeffry You heard. You're going to lick these. See. Every inch. See. Aren't you?

Dennis Am I heck. Yes, alright, I am.

Jeffry I'm going to keep a punishment book for you from now on. Right? Naughty boys have to be kept in order.

Dennis What'll you do?

Jeffry That depends. You'll have to wait and see.

Dennis Go on. Tell us.

Jeffry No.

Dennis Please.

Jeffry I'll do it now if you're not careful.

Dennis I'd like to see you try.

Jeffry Come here then.

Dennis Gerroff.

Jeffry Shall I take my belt off to you?

Dennis No. Now stop it.

Jeffry (*takes his belt off*) Right then. You asked for it.

   Dennis giggles.

Now own up. You deserve it, don't you?

   Dennis giggles.

Now take your medicine. There's a good boy. Come on, hold still. (*Hits him.*) Don't it hurt. (*Hits again.*) Want more?

Dennis Here, that's enough. That's enough. Don't go bloody mad.

Jeffry There. That was for nothing. Now do something.

Dennis I still think you've got a slate off.

Jeffry Now don't push your luck. I don't want to have to take it off to you again. Do I?

Dennis You'll have to catch me first.

Jeffry Listen. What's that?

Dennis A cat.

Jeffry Come on.

Dennis What?

Jeffry Come on. Get it.

Dennis We can't get it.

Jeffry Come on. Are you game?

Dennis Listen.

Jeffry There it is. They've had it doctored. Look at it.

Dennis I'm not.

Jeffry You are.

Dennis I'm not.

Jeffry You are.

Dennis Aren't they delicate?

Jeffry You get it.

Dennis I can't.

Jeffry Get it. Go on. Use my coat. Come on. Bring it over the allotments.

SCENE EIGHT

The following takes place simultaneously:

Mother Then of course there was the terrible murder of Bobby Kennedy. I don't think I could have felt worse if he was related to me. All those lovely children left fatherless. Such a good man too. I cried myself sick, in fact we were all crying, Arthur was having a little weep as well, wasn't it dreadful, dear, two lovely young men murdered, the poor parents and wives and the boy helping to carry his father's coffin. God comfort them all.

Father (*reads an article of his own choice from the day's newspaper*)

Mrs B (*folding baby's clothes and smoking*) There, that's better.

93

They stop.

Dennis The bell goes for the last lap and then your heart is going inside you. You can see it. (*Pulses his hand.*) And you are running after it. It's going so powerfully, you know it will break open. It's bloody hideous. You remember it dormant. How it pulsed sly. (*Imitates with his hand.*) Your chest is still burning. You hope your heart is as strong as it feels. As it still feels. The bell goes for the last lap. Ah. Ah. Aah. Ah. Beautiful it's been, the run. You know how. You are going through it. But you don't know what own you will come into when you have broken through what it is you will break into, what from what of what. All the bloody effort gone. Now it's bad. And go. And go. Don't last too long. Then: don't last no longer. And then: not much longer. Don't last. It

Jeffry (*feeding the baby with a bottle*) Come on. Here we are. Oh, it's a bit hot. (*Tests it on his arm.*) Here we are. Come on. Don't you want any? Eh? Look it's lovely. (*He tastes it.*) Now you. No? No? Come on, you've got to eat you know. Thirsty. Thirsty. Thirsty. (*Tests it again.*) Just right. (*The baby feeds.*) You were thirsty, weren't you? That's what you were. Do you want winding? (*Picks the baby up.*)

will be longer. Please.
Please. The end. Let me.
Sick. This is the worst.
There was nothing.
It was only over.
This isn't nothing. You
have stopped. That. In it.
On the ground. Your
chest is burnt out. Back
in you, your heart is
throwing itself about.
The grass is unwelcoming.
Breathing. Sore. Sobbing.
Actually. You quieten.
And automatically have
wrapped up. Who did you
cuddle? It's cool. It will
rain. No one is really, even
through the cheering. Sweat
cools on your forehead.
There's those programmes
on the empty parts of the
stands. This is me. Why
did I do that? What
legs am I walking on?
Aching enjoyable. I ran.
Oh dear. What was
all that in aid of?

*Mother, Father and Mrs B repeat what they said
previously.*

SCENE NINE

A Co-operative Wholesale Society store. The shoe department.

Dennis I don't know what we have to come here for in the first place.

Mother What's wrong with the Co-op? I've shopped here for years.

Dennis You look like it an' all.

Mother Now don't be difficult, Dennis. I've got a bad head.

Dennis What did you come here for then?

Mother I thought I was going to be alright. And I thought you wanted a pair of shoes.

Dennis I did. I don't see why we have to come here though. Look at them. I'm not having anything like that, I can tell you.

Mother You can't beat a good Wheatsheaf shoe.

Dennis That's what you think.

Mother Look, Lord Muck, when you can pay for your own shoes, then we'll go where you want, alright? Where's the assistant?

Dennis Serving someone down there.

Mother Do you feel hot?

Dennis Not particularly.

Mother I shouldn't have come out. Especially with a bloody great kid like you. Where are you going now? Now don't wander off. That man'll be here in a minute. Oh my God, I feel bad. Dennis.

Dennis What?

Mother Come back here. Here, give me your arm. Let me hold on to you. I feel giddy. Oh dear!

Dennis Shut up, Mam. People will see you. Are you alright, Mam? Don't show me up. Mam.

Mother Ask them to get me a drink of water, Dennis.

Dennis I can't.

Mother It's alright. It's passed over, I think. You wait. I'll tell your father when I get home.

Dennis Tell who you like.

Enter the Assistant.

Assistant Now then.

Dennis Shoes please. Size 8.

Assistant Colour?

Dennis I don't know. What do you think?

Mother Brown.

Assistant And what style were you thinking of?

Mother A nice pair of lace-ups, I think.

Dennis No!

Assistant Certainly, I'll see what I can find. (*He goes.*)

Dennis Are you alright? Ay? Are you feeling a bit better?

Mother A lot you seem to care.

Dennis Oh, don't start.

Mother You always used to be such a nice boy, Dennis.

Dennis Oh, leave me alone.

Mother I'll have to have a drink of water. My head's really bad.

Dennis Well, I don't know where to get one.

Mother You'll be sorry, Dennis, you behaved like this after I'm dead.

Dennis You'd be better off dead if you're going to be ill like this all the time.

Mother I shall have to go to the Ladies.

Dennis What am I going to do?

Mother Here, hold the shopping bag and don't go wandering off. (*Exits.*)

Enter Assistant.

Assistant Where's your mammy?

Dennis She's gone, you know. In there.

Assistant Well, we'd better try these, hadn't we? How's that?

Dennis Alright, I think.

Assistant Are they too tight?

Dennis They are a bit.

Assistant Well, walk about on it. Are they comfortable?

Dennis I don't know.

Assistant Well, if you don't, I don't. Would you like to try these on?

Dennis Oh. OK.

Assistant Here, now. (*Pinches the toes.*) They seem nice and easy. How are they across here?

Dennis Oh! I've just remembered.

Assistant What?

Dennis I haven't got any money. She's got her purse with her.

Assistant Well, she'll be back.

Dennis I expect so. I'd better wait for her.

Assistant What's your name?

Dennis Dennis.

Assistant Oh, yes. I suppose I'd better put these away then. There's no peace, is there? And you'd better wait for your mammy.

Dennis Well, I think I'll wait for her outside.

Assistant Alright, please yourself. Bye-bye, Dennis.

Enter Mother.

Dennis Are you any better?

Mother Not much.

Dennis You look awful red.

Mother Do I?

Dennis Shall we go home?

Mother I think I'll have to. What about your shoes?

Dennis Never mind about them. I'll come in on my own one day.

SCENE TEN

Jeffry comes in with Dennis riding on his shoulders.

Jeffry Ee. Ee. Ee. Here he is. Here he is. Here he is.

Dennis Let me down, Jeffry. Jeffry? Put me down, you silly sod. People'll hear you.

Jeffry Come on then, let's have a look at the swag. Open your carrier. Go on, open it.

 Dennis does so.

What did you get? Here, that's nice. (*taking out women's clothing*) You can have that.

Dennis Cheeky sod!

Jeffry Oo. Oo. Oo. Drawers.

Dennis Put 'em back.

Jeffry What do we do with them?

Dennis I don't know.

Jeffry Bury them.

Dennis What for?

Jeffry Well, we can't keep them, can we?

Dennis I don't know.

Jeffry Well, we can't. We'll have to dig a hole and cover them. Let's go over the gun-post. Bring 'em with you.

Dennis What for?

Jeffry I like it over there. Come on.

SCENE ELEVEN

A gun-shelter.

Jeffry This is where they used to fire. Ack. Ack. Ack. See the shooting range. Let's go and jump off it.

Dennis I'm scared.

Jeffry No. It's not high. You climb up the steps, walk along and jump down. Jump. Climb up the steps, walk along the parapet and jump down.

Both (*together*) Climb, walk along and jump down.

   They go into the shelter.

Jeffry You can see the sea from here. Look.

Dennis Oh, aye, so you can.

Jeffry Come on. Get it out.

Dennis What?

Jeffry Let's see it.

Dennis No.

Jeffry Come on.

Dennis No. Get out. (*He goes on to the top again.*)

Jeffry Alright then. Yellow. Shit-scared. (*He comes out.*) Ack. Ack. Ack. (*He pisses against the wall.*) That's better. Let's see if I can write your name in it.

Dennis I should like to set fire to this city. Starting over there. I'd like it to be on a hot day like today when the whole place is at its feeble best. Look over there. Look at it. It is like a cave with burrows. Full at night with a few old tom cats. Perhaps I died then. I had a sudden feeling.

I want to be in extreme situations. I want to be in the death cell or in the gas chamber. I'd like to kill you. I wish you'd kill me.

Jeffry I'll kill you.

Dennis Come on then, kill me.

Jeffry I'll kill you. You'd be scared silly if I really did touch you.

Dennis Would I?

Jeffry Yes, you would.

Dennis Would I?

Jeffry Yes, you would would.

Dennis Yes, I would. I'm dead anyway. I wish you'd let me rest. You do sometimes. That's when I'm not with you.

Jeffry I think you're fucking potty, you are.

Dennis I'm not, I'm dead.

Jeffry You're there.

Dennis I died in 1947.

Jeffry You wasn't even born in 1947. That's got you.

Dennis I know. Funny, isn't it?

They go into the gun-shelter.

Dennis My mother's dying, I think.

Jeffry Get out, she's not.

Dennis How do you know?

Jeffry Well, I bet she's not.

Dennis I don't care what you think.

Jeffry Is she? I'm sorry to hear that. I am. What's the matter? She had her breast off?

Dennis No, it's her kidneys, the doctor said. What's that on your hand?

Jeffry has the word LOVE *tattooed on the backs of the fingers of one of his hands.*

Is it true what you told me about your landlady?

Jeffry What?

Dennis You know.

Jeffry Of course I fuck my landlady. Of course. What do you think I do? I go for older women generally. Quite scraggy old birds. What a way to spend Saturday night. It's months since I've had me end off. Still, it's Sunday tomorrer. I love all the little birds in their curlers on a Sunday morning after having been shagged stiff on the Saturday night. I bet you're a right little shagger, ain't yer!

Dennis When my mother took me into the Ladies lavatory with her when we were out, she used to give me her handbag to hold. Then. Piss. Piss. Piss. I used to look into it. 'Don't look into my handbag, Dennis, I've told you before. Handbags are private property. I've given it to you for you to hold it.' Sometimes when she didn't go outside she would shut the door to the kitchen and use a bowl. I could hear her through in the other room. She had this same handbag for years. She used to keep in it, besides all her own things, my birth certificate and the club books.

Jeffry Don't she now?

Dennis She's dead.

Jeffry She's not. I've seen her.

Dennis That's not my mother.

Jeffry Get out. I never seen much of my mother after I was twelve.

Dennis How's that?

Jeffry Well, I went away to school then, didn't I? She should never have let them took me.

Dennis Well, she couldn't have done anything about it, I suppose.

Jeffry You shut up. What do you know about it? I only took two oranges.

Dennis That's what you say.

Jeffry True as I'm sat here.

Dennis The first time.

Jeffry Yeah. (*Pause.*) They lie there, you know. Like a vampire that's had a stake drove through its heart. Without the stake. (*Pause.*) The lavatory pan in our house was cracked. My father was straining at the leash when he had a stroke. The pan cracked right across. He died. There were big turds left in the base of it. He must have been a giant. Come on, let's go over the foreshore.

Dennis No.

Jeffry The boy next door to us picks coal over there.

Dennis Rather him than me.

Jeffry Makes a fortune.

Dennis Bloody Dickensian.

Jeffry Come on.

Dennis I'm fed up.

Jeffry You going home?

Dennis I don't know.

Jeffry I think you're half ginger, you are. Eh? Aren't you though? Answer me. Aren't you though? Oh, please yourself.

Dennis You going over there then?

Jeffry Yes.

Dennis I'm not.

Jeffry You go home, kid.

Dennis No, I'm coming.

Jeffry No, you go on home . . . go on.

Dennis Tara then.

Jeffry So long.

SCENE TWELVE

Father having his tea. Enter Dennis.

Dennis Where's Mam?

Father She's upstairs. She's poorly, she's having a lie-down.

Dennis What's the matter. Is she alright? Have you had the doctor?

Father Don't be silly, son. She's only got a sick headache. She's having a rest with the curtains drawn.

Dennis Mam, Mam, are you alright?

Father Let her alone, Dennis. Or pop up and see her quiet, like a good lad.

Dennis No, I don't want to. I'll go up afterwards.

Father I'll get you your tea. She's put it out for you.

Dennis What's she want to go to bed for? She knows I haven't had my tea. She's always the same, she is.

Father Now just you be still. Do you hear me? You're growing daft, you are. Sit to the table.

Dennis sits.

Dennis It's nicer down here without her anyway. Can I have more biscuits?

Father No, you can't. You don't want them, you eat what you've got first. (*Pause.*) You can come and help me out there after. (*pointing to garden*)

Dennis You must be mad. Catch me out there.

Father Pass me the *Echo*, son. Why don't you take your mother up a cup of tea? (*Pause.*) Here. I see old Georgie Green's wife's died. Your mother'll be sorry to hear that. Yesterday. At home. Funeral Wednesday. Gentlemen only. I'm working. Pass us the milk, Dennis. How much milk does she like?

Dennis Just a bit.

Father (*goes back to paper*) A cat. A ginger tom cat was found recently on an allotment at Morpeth Estate. Hanging by a piece of string from a bean pole. The damage is believed to have been done by vandals or boys. The tenants' association have lodged a complaint. That it is possible for unauthorised entry. Here, that must have been that cat up the road. Your mother said they'd missed it. Bloody young thugs. A nice well-kept bloody animal like that. Are you going to take it up, or shall I?

Dennis I will.

Father Go on, then.

The End.

SMALL CHANGE

Small Change was first produced at the Royal Court Theatre, London, in July 1976. It was revived, in repertory with *Kick for Touch*, on the Cottesloe stage of the National Theatre, London, on 23 February 1983, with the following cast:

Gerard James Hazeldine
Mrs Harte June Watson
Vincent Philip Joseph
Mrs Driscoll Marjorie Yates,
    Maggie Steed (Cottesloe Theatre)

Directed by Peter Gill

Characters

Gerard

Mrs Harte

Vincent

Mrs Driscoll

The action takes place mainly on
the East Side of Cardiff.

None of the characters leaves the stage.

One

Gerard It was clean. I make that up. But it was. I'll make it up. It was clean. Distempered walls with a paper border, an oval mirror, oil-cloth, a negro money-box, picture of the King . . . In the other house everything was worse. The smell was worse. Medals of grease on the rugs. Tea leaves and bits and leavings outside the drain, etc . . . And there was a garden front and back. Two photographs show that. And I know there were roses. In one photograph, a woman standing in front of the house. In one of the photographs, a woman is standing behind an iron gate on the path in front of the house, with this bundle, this child, in this young scowling woman's arms. Thick ankles, strap shoes, a pinafore, cropped hair . . .

Mrs Harte We were all young, with young families, and you could walk over the tide-field to the channel. Cut a few sandwiches for the children's tea and then, when the men come home, they'd walk over and we'd all stroll back together. I don't know what we moved for – three bedrooms and a front room, and that was empty very nigh eighteen months with nothing kept in it but the bike. There was an air-strip over there during the war. I used to stand in the landing window waiting for the siren to go, and look out, nursing you old-fashioned style, if I was in the house by myself. Do you remember the German plane that made a landing there? I never had such a fright in all my life. Then after that they built a big wind tunnel there. That was an awful noise too. Rover cars have got it now, I'm told. Uncle picked coal over there when he was a child. You ask him. On the foreshore next to Guest Keen's. You ask him about the time he was over there with Jimmy Harrington, when my mother thought they were lost and went looking for them. And when she found them she leathered them all the way home with their wet stockings. What? Oh, he was a lovely boy, Jimmy Harrington. Oh, he really was. He was lost at sea. The war finished me off. It started everything, and it ended everything.

Vincent There was a wind when I turned the corner, blowing down the main road. There was no one in front of me. It was nearly dark. Blokes from the steel works, all covered in red dust, passed me on their way home, pedalling very hard and slow against the wind. Everything went red as they tipped slag on to the foreshore. When they do that, suddenly, without a sound, the sky goes red. It was a cold night, aye, but I was soon at the corner of the street. I slung my coat over the banisters and went into the living room. Across the backs, lights through the curtains made the windows different colours. I turned on the wireless and sat down to take my boots off, putting them by the sofa. My dinner was on a saucepan being kept warm for me in the kitchen. I brought my plate in with a cloth and moved my place into the middle of the table, starting to eat before I was sat down. The potatoes were scorching. I was finished in no time. I wiped my plate clean with a bit of bread and pushed the plate away from me. Cor, the potatoes had been so hot they'd nearly burned me. Phew. I got up from the table and sat on the sofa. I didn't want to be too near the fire. I fancied a cup of tea but I felt too full from eating too quick. And too tired after work. I switched the radio over and then I switched it off. Through the wall, I could hear the wireless next door playing dance music. I went outside to the outside toilet.

When I come back I could see next door's curtains weren't drawn. The music was so loud you could hear it out there. A little boy about . . . I don't know. Must have been about . . . I could see him in the room dancing to the music, all by himself, like a little girl. No, not like a little girl. He was just like a little boy. I watched him in the cold. It was too.

Gerard He was sitting opposite me. He sat sprawled, legs apart, nursing a bottle of Irish whiskey inside his shirt, next to his chest. I look like my mother in every way except for her hair, he said. You've got it. He leant forward, grabbing. Where did you get it, he said. Oh Jesus . . . I told him.

Vincent I eased the middle of the banked-up fire open to see its red inside and to encourage it to burn its covering of small coal. Hung over it, poker in my hand, I destroyed shapes that the burning coal was making, watched it forming a new mass, and then destroyed that. I tested my forearm, holding it before the heat. The wireless next door was still playing. I was hot. I wondered whether or not to let the fire die down. Someone had built it up to keep it in.

Mrs Harte The war finished me off. It started everything and it ended everything.

Gerard Whose face did my grin start on? On what face will it end? I seek desperately to find resemblances – her eyes there, her manner there, her punishing, unacknowledged, defensive aah . . . What is it, what is it that will, will find the moment, that will . . . What is it, what is it that will, will find the moment, that will . . .? Did a woman ever live who wasn't slowly killing herself, smoothing her backside lightly as if going to sit down and saying, I'm all bleeding?

Mrs Driscoll Your legs get cold just nipping across the back like that. I'll have to go.

Mrs Harte Sit down, you've only just come in.

Mrs Driscoll No, I can't.

Mrs Harte Come on, sit down.

Mrs Driscoll I mustn't be long. Oh, I don't know what to do with myself.

Mrs Harte Who's got the baby?

Mrs Driscoll I don't know what I'm going to do, I really don't. (*She weeps bitterly.*)

Mrs Harte There we are.

Mrs Driscoll I kept our Eileen home. She's taken him out. Michael has gone down our Julie's.

Mrs Harte Will you have a cup of tea?

Mrs Driscoll No, I can't stay.

Mrs Harte You feel bad?

Mrs Driscoll I feel really bad. I'm in the middle of black-leading the grate. I can't even work it off. He can be so nice when he wants. He was out till gone quarter to twelve last night. I don't know where he could have been to that time. He was ever so abusive when I asked him. He stood in that doorway there, in that overcoat, awfully unsteady. He wouldn't say. He never does.

Mrs Harte I wouldn't give him the pleasure of asking. I should have been in bed if it were me. You must want your head read, waiting up to that time.

Mrs Driscoll It's no good, I can't go to sleep if I'm in bed on my own. And then when he's in that state I can't go to sleep either.

Mrs Harte Let mine lie by me drunk, he'd be on the oil-cloth in the morning.

Mrs Driscoll He hung his coat on a hook in the passage and nearly twenty pounds fell out of it.

Mrs Harte I hope it's in yours now.

Mrs Driscoll Oh, I couldn't.

Mrs Harte You should have snaffled it. How would he know? Drunken old bugger.

Mrs Driscoll Oh, I couldn't.

Mrs Harte Well of all the silly, soft . . . How would he ever know? He could have lost it anywhere.

Mrs Driscoll I wouldn't be able to carry it off.

Mrs Harte The two-timing, bloody, conniving old get. He wants a good kicking.

Mrs Driscoll I don't think you should say that kind of thing.

Mrs Harte Well, I wouldn't invite it then.

Mrs Driscoll I'd better be going. I'm all on edge. You won't say anything? I'm sorry. I don't know what to do. Honestly, Mrs Harte, I wish I could pack it all in.

Mrs Harte Eh, eh, eh, eh. That's enough of that.

Mrs Driscoll The house is getting me down. I can't keep up with it.

Mrs Harte Well, may God forgive you.

Mrs Driscoll Do you know, I never used to suffer like that. Do you know, once upon a time I never knew what it was to miss a night's sleep. Now it's like hell on earth.

Mrs Harte I know. I generally sleep all right, I must say. If I don't, it's like hell itself.

Mrs Driscoll I lie there. I've got this habit of clenching my hands. And sweating. I can't keep still. But you have to when he has to be up so early. It's all my fault. It's my fault. I think it's my fault, see.

Mrs Harte What is?

Mrs Driscoll It *is*. Do you know . . . Well, you know, Mrs Harte, I never . . . You know . . . I never went out with anyone before I met John. Well not . . . You know.

Mrs Harte I should hope not.

Mrs Driscoll The windows all need cleaning. I cleaned the mirror once today. Now there's finger marks all over it again.

Mrs Harte Well, what does that matter?

Mrs Driscoll The children's shoes all need mending. *He* mends them usually. We've got a last.

Mrs Harte Won't he do them then?

Mrs Driscoll Yes. Only I don't know *when* he's going to do them. I just wish they was done. It's all a mess, wherever you look. You finish something. You turn around and nothing's been done. And you notice everything. I get up, I think, another day.

Mrs Harte Blimey, who doesn't think that? Here goes another day. Let's get 'em all out of it. Let's have a sit down. That's the way I think. It's wrong, I know. And then when they're gone, I get lonely. But as soon as they're in again I think, Oh, Christ, why don't you all go out and leave me alone?

Mrs Driscoll I'm all right, when I start working. If I can just get through it, I don't know. It's wicked – to feel like this, isn't it? Don't you think? It must be, I think.

Mrs Harte What in the name of Jesus is wicked about it?

Mrs Driscoll Oh it is. And I used to be ever such a good manager.

Mrs Harte Oh don't talk so soft. Don't you think everyone feels like that? I do.

Mrs Driscoll And I think I'm late.

Mrs Harte Oh, now my God Almighty. Are you sure?

Mrs Driscoll Yes. No. I don't know. I'm not certain sure.

Mrs Harte Well then.

Mrs Driscoll I'm pretty sure.

Mrs Harte Can you tell?

Mrs Driscoll Generally.

Mrs Harte Well *you're* lucky. I never can. How long?

Mrs Driscoll I don't know.

Mrs Harte Well, we'll hope.

Mrs Driscoll Yes.

Mrs Harte Dear dear, I dunno.

Mrs Driscoll I'll have to go in, it's the rent man today.

Mrs Harte I know.

Mrs Driscoll I owe him three weeks.

Mrs Harte Well I don't know what I'm going to do. I think I'll be ready for the hurry-up wagon at this rate.

Mrs Driscoll Oh, Mrs Harte, I wish he loved me.

Mrs Harte Don't be silly, of course he does.

Mrs Driscoll I think he does in his way – do you?

Mrs Harte Don't be silly, of course he does. (*as though the subject was embarrassing and out of place*) Come on now, you're a young woman.

Mrs Driscoll If only he'd love me I'd be all right. I would. I don't care about the kids, that's the God's truth and I can't help it, I can't. I've only got any feeling for him, isn't it awful, only him. I don't want anything else in the whole world. I wish the kids were dead and me with them. It's half killing me. I followed him into town last Saturday. I left the kids with our Vincent. He's a good kid. He went right into the Park Hotel.

Mrs Harte The mean old sod. Did you go in after him?

Mrs Driscoll I couldn't. I didn't have no stockings on. I only had a pair of our Eileen's school socks on. I just went out on the spur. Put my coat on over my pinafore. Who does he go to meet in a place like that?

Mrs Harte Which bar did he go in?

Mrs Driscoll I don't know.

Mrs Harte Well, you were soft. I expect he just went in for a drink. You're making too much of it. You don't give yourself the chance to think about anything else. You should get out more. (*listening*) There's the baby.

Mrs Driscoll I'll have to go in.

Mrs Harte He'll be all right.

Mrs Driscoll No, I'd better go in.

Mrs Harte Come and have a lie down in here for the afternoon.

Mrs Driscoll No, I'll have to get the tea on.

Mrs Harte Oh, don't mind the tea, come in here.

Mrs Driscoll No, no, I'm feeling a bit better now. Thanks.

Mrs Harte Well, bang on the wall if you want me.

Vincent She used to sit rubbing her ankles, pulling the curl out of her hair, and straightening it behind her ears. She used to sit as if she was warming herself. She used to sit reading her woman's paper. She used to sit, crying, bitter.

Mrs Driscoll I have been in worse states and I must have faith that I'll get through this one, and so on for better or worse. And that the end will be better or worse. But it will be different, being the end.

Gerard Over the tide-field. Past dismantled allotments. Currant bushes run to seed with flowers growing in them from seed blown into them. Bits of the war. Targets. Gun posts. The sand pit. The cinder track ends in turf. Pull up a tuft of coarse grass to see if there's a curlew nest. Nothing there. That's where they lay eggs. Lie by the river. Steep, gleaming mud. Wide empty river and then in no time a full tide, swelling, catching the sun. Lie, looking up to catch a skylark. River at full flood. Slip into it. Cattle marooned on the grass island. Afraid to swim that far. Duck and float. Slide out on to the turf, and lie, hoping to catch a skylark. Then walking fast, skirting the marsh, cracking the salty reeds, walk along the trenches, cut to drain the whole field, until at last the estuary. The grasses on the bank laden with sand like snow. Watch it spread. And then the channel. The sea catching everything, swallowing everything, taking everything with it and just leaving behind a coarse rim of gritty soil. Sky goes red. When they tip slag on the foreshore, the whole place floods red. Bright weather again. Back to streets.

Mrs Harte Where have you been?

Gerard Over the tide.

Mrs Harte You wanna be careful.

Gerard Yeah.

Mrs Harte You been swimming?

Gerard I had a dip.

Mrs Harte Oh, don't.

Vincent It's all right, it's me.

Mrs Driscoll Is that you?

Vincent What?

Mrs Driscoll Is that you?

Vincent Yes. Where's the kids? Where's Eileen? What's the matter?

Mrs Driscoll Nothing. Where have you been?

Vincent There is. Mam? What's the matter? Where is everybody?

Mrs Driscoll Shut up. She's taken them out.

Vincent What's the matter then?

Mrs Driscoll Where have you been?

Vincent What is it, Mam? Come on, tell us.

Mrs Driscoll Where have you been?

Vincent I been for a swim. What's the matter?

Mrs Driscoll Where?

Vincent What is it?

Mrs Driscoll Where have you been?

Vincent Over the tide. Over the tide. All right? I been for a swim. The tide's in.

Mrs Harte Where have you been?

Gerard Out.

Mrs Harte I know you been out. Where out?

Gerard Over the East Dock, for a swim.

Mrs Harte Oh, don't. It's so dangerous.

Mrs Driscoll Have you been swimming?

Vincent Yeah.

Mrs Driscoll Have you been over the Dock? Have you? You wait till your father comes in.

Gerard I been over the tide.

Mrs Harte I know, your hair's wet. Was the tide up? Was it? Eh?

Gerard Of course it was.

Mrs Harte I wish I had a paper, I'd look. Was it?

Gerard Yes, I said.

Mrs Harte It better have been.

Gerard Where you going?

Vincent I got to go in.

Gerard Oh.

Vincent Where *you* going?

Gerard I got to go in.

Vincent Well, what's the matter with you then? Eh? Mmmm?

Gerard I'm going in then, OK. OK?

Vincent All right then, go in.

Gerard You going in?

Vincent Yeah.

Gerard I got to have my tea.

Vincent All right then.

Gerard Call for us later then.

Vincent OK.

Gerard Don't forget. Vincent. Vincent!

Vincent I won't forget. Go on. I'll see you later.

Gerard Where you going? I thought you was going in?

Vincent I got to do my paper round first.

Gerard You've done your paper round.

Vincent I haven't. I didn't do it.

Gerard Do you want me to come with you then?

Vincent No, I'm not doing it.

Gerard Why not?

Vincent I don't feel like it. All right? Anyway, I'm packing it in.

Gerard Where you going then?

Vincent I don't know. I thought you had to go in. Go on. I'll see you later.

Gerard No you won't.

Vincent All right then. What's the matter with you? Eh? Mmmm? All right then.

Gerard Nothing's the matter with me.

Vincent Well then, go in then.

Gerard I am going in.

Vincent I'm going in an' all.

Gerard Don't go in.

Vincent I got to.

Gerard And me.

Vincent I'll see you later.

Gerard Aye. Don't forget.

Mrs Driscoll Vincent!

Mrs Harte Come here, let me look at you. Come here. Why are your shorts buttoned like that? Where have you been?

Gerard Out playing.

Mrs Harte I know. Where have you been?

Gerard Out the back. Down the shelter.

Mrs Harte Who with?

Gerard With Vincent.

Mrs Harte Come here.

Gerard No.

Mrs Harte Come here.

Gerard (*giggling*) No.

Mrs Harte Come here, till I split you. What were you doing? Come here.

Gerard Playing.

Mrs Harte Come here.

Gerard (*giggling*) No.

Mrs Harte Wait till I catch hold of you.

Gerard With Vincent.

Mrs Harte Come here. Gerard.

Gerard I'm going out. Tara.

Mrs Harte Gerard.

Vincent Gerard.

Gerard What?

Vincent Got any?

Gerard What?

Vincent Seen any nests?

Gerard I'm stuck.

Vincent What d'you mean?

Gerard Are you stuck?

Vincent Of course I'm not stuck. What do you mean, stuck? How can you be stuck? I've just stopped, that's all.

Gerard Don't look down. I'm stuck.

Vincent What? Blimey. Come down, come down.

Gerard I can't.

Vincent Oh, blimey.

Gerard Don't come up.

Vincent Blimey. Well climb on up. Go on.

Gerard I can't.

Vincent Well, come on down.

Gerard I can't.

Vincent Blimey. It was you went up there. You went up there. What do you want to go up there for?

Gerard Don't look down.

Vincent Why not? (*He looks down.*) Blimey!

Gerard Here's the dock coppers.

Vincent Oh Christ. Come on. Come down.

Gerard I can't.

Gerard Or earlier. Lost, crawling up the beach, under the legs of tethered beach ponies. Short beaten horses. Shore, ribbed like the roof of a huge mouth. The grey sea filling abandoned holes. Ma ma ma Mam . . .

Mrs Harte What have you got there? What have you got in your hand? Come on – give it to me. Sweet paper. Throw it down. I'll slap you hard. Here, hold my bag.

Vincent You coming over the field, Ger?

Gerard No, I can't.

Vincent Why not?

Gerard I can't get through the barbed wire.

Vincent Yes, you can. Come on.

Mrs Driscoll Where have you been?

Gerard Perhaps I'd been over the park, or into town, or with Vincent, or out, or lying under the tree. Or down the field, lying under the tree, eating banana sandwiches or hanging about or deliberately wasting time, deliberately creating tedium. Or over the park, having squeezed through the railings rather than go through the gate, and having squeezed through the railings, climbed up and sat on the railway embankment, above the bushes and birch trees, and looked down onto the soccer pitches and having walked along the line above the playground, sat above the other pitches and seen the whole plan of the park. Or gone for a swim in the park baths. Through the green turnstile, hoping for a single cubicle, to avoid other boys. Boys changing in cubicles without doors. Boys with lamed legs. Boys flicking towels. Afraid to stand near the deep end, for fear of being pushed in. Grazed knee on the concrete of the pool. Was the sting from the chlorine or the concrete grazing the skin off? Polio scares. Or over the playground. Sometimes the swings are wrapped round the top of the supports by the big boys, youths, thugs. Teds, youths, roughs, vandals now. Swinging, frightened someone will push you so high that you have to jump off or it's too late and you are afraid to jump off. There's a moment when the swing stops, with a curious kind of gulp in the chain. You could go so high you could swing right over and crash down. The older boys are standing on the seats, girls sitting between them, between their legs and feet, bending at the knees to get an impetus to swing higher. The parkie driving them away. Cheeking him. Hooligans. I forgot.

Vincent Do you want a lift, Gerard?

Mrs Harte You're not giving him a lift. I've told you two before. About that. On the handlebars. I saw you.

Vincent Only on the bar, Mrs Harte.

Mrs Harte No.

Gerard No, you go on. I'm not going this afternoon.

Mrs Harte What did you say?

Gerard You heard.

Mrs Harte What did you say?

Gerard You heard that, too.

Mrs Harte Come here, I'll cleave you, you little get.

Gerard I'm not feeling well. I can't go back.

Mrs Harte On your way. And you too, Vincent. Off you go.

Gerard I'm not going.

Mrs Harte You are.

Gerard I'm not.

Mrs Harte Oh, oh, but you are.

Gerard Oh, but I'm not.

Mrs Harte Now, get your blazer.

Gerard I feel sick.

Mrs Harte So do I. Where is it?

Gerard Blazer!

Mrs Harte That's a nice blazer.

Gerard You wear it, then.

Mrs Harte Come here.

Vincent I'm going, then.

Gerard Yeah. You go on.

Mrs Harte He's coming now, Vincent. Get your blazer. Now get it.

Gerard I don't know where it is.

Mrs Harte Find it. Upstairs.

Gerard It isn't upstairs.

Vincent I'm going then.

Mrs Harte I'm not writing you a note, so don't think I am.

Gerard That's OK by me.

Mrs Harte You're a hateful kid.

Vincent Tara.

Gerard Anyway, I'm leaving.

Mrs Harte I wish you could bloody leave. The sooner the better. But you're not leaving. Right. Dear dear. You'd better go, Vincent.

Vincent Tara then.

Gerard What's the matter?

Vincent I'm going then.

Gerard What's the matter?

Mrs Harte Nothing's the matter. I'm sick of you, that's all, you little swine. I am. Honest to God, I am. You're tiring me out.

Gerard All right, I'll go.

Mrs Harte I don't care if you do go.

Gerard All right, I'm not going.

Mrs Harte And I'm not writing you a note.

Gerard Don't worry, I'll write one myself.

Mrs Harte Oh, Jesus, help me with this swine of a kid.

Vincent I'm going then.

Gerard Look at it.

Mrs Harte What?

Gerard All of it. In here. Out there. The street. I'm fed up. I'm fed up.

Mrs Harte You're fed up. That's a laugh. You're bloody fed up. A kid of your age. I'm fed up to the back teeth, I am.

Gerard *And* I'm bored.

Mrs Harte Bored. What you bored with then? Eh? Eh?

Gerard Oh, nothing, nothing. I'm going.

Mrs Harte Where?

Gerard Oh, I don't know. School.

Mrs Harte You'd better run for it then.

Gerard Or perhaps I'd been over the park. Seen the old man with his plastic shopping bag and sandwiches for his favourite children. Or gone down the other end, the nice end, with the dilapidated tennis courts and garden and bowling green fielding old men with flannels and cream jackets and rubber overshoes, with their rubber mats. Boring, unavoidable, glimpses of peace, with their gardens, and allotments, pipes. Unendurable visions of their perfect lives. Gardens, cars, good sense, polished furniture, kindliness. Their dullness and their humour killing me. Clerks in the Inland Revenue, with established posts or perhaps retired, with daughters and a son with a car. Holidays. Two weeks. Rockeries. Kindly good sense. Delivered papers. *Everybody's, News Chronicle, Herald. Reynolds News?* Hardly. Perhaps. Radio with pleated silk, backing the fretwork. Anonymous, once pretty wives. With their prudence and irritating passions and have been in the war.

Mrs Driscoll Aren't you going out, Vincent? Vincent?

Vincent No.

Mrs Driscoll Don't you have to go to church tonight?

Gerard Don't forget I'm on the altar tonight, Mam. Mam.

Vincent No.

Mrs Harte What?

Gerard Don't forget, will you?

Mrs Harte (*imitating his whine*) Don't forget.

Mrs Driscoll Well, don't sulk in here, Vincent.

Gerard I wants a clean cotta, mind.

Mrs Harte Do you? Well you can want on.

Gerard Aw, Mam.

Mrs Driscoll Stop spitting, Vincent. There's a good boy. It's a terrible habit you've got. Are you sure you're not meant to be going to church?

Gerard Mam.

Mrs Harte You had it clean on on Sunday. Anyway you didn't bring it home in time.

Gerard I did. I brought it home yesterday.

Mrs Harte Yesterday.

Gerard Well, will you iron it then?

Mrs Harte No, I won't bloody iron it. On your way.

Mrs Driscoll It's Wednesday night, Vincent. I'm sure you're supposed to be in church.

Mrs Harte And I'm not washing any more football gear either. Right?

Gerard Right.

Mrs Harte You cheeky . . . Come here. Come here, till I kill you.

Mrs Driscoll Vincent.

Vincent Oh Christ. I'm going out.

Mrs Driscoll What did you say? Vincent.

Vincent Tara.

Mrs Driscoll Vincent. What did you say, Vincent!

Mrs Harte Come here.

Mrs Driscoll Vincent!

Mrs Harte There's Vincent. Come in, Vincent. You going to Benediction? If you are I hope you're in a better frame of mind than him.

Vincent No.

Mrs Harte I bet he doesn't keep on about clean cottas.

Gerard Why don't you do a swop?

Mrs Harte I wish to Christ I could.

Gerard Anyway, he doesn't need a clean cotta, that's why.

Mrs Harte Because he keeps his clean, I should think.

Gerard No, clever, he got chucked off.

Mrs Harte Get out, he never did, did you, Vincent? What for?

Gerard His face don't fit.

Mrs Harte Now, shut it, you. There's favouritism down there. Right through the bloody parish. Nice Catholics some of them are.

Gerard That's what I said.

Mrs Harte I'll do for you in a minute.

Gerard Come on. Come on.

Mrs Harte Now stop it.

Gerard Come on.

Mrs Harte Go on, go on. Get out, get out. Ooh, I've hurt my arm now.

Gerard Have you? Come on. What's the matter?

Mrs Harte I'm not talking to you.

Gerard Why not?

Mrs Harte You've got no respect. Go on, the pair of you.

Gerard Where you going?

Vincent I'll walk down with you.

Mrs Harte And don't you be late. Do you hear?

Gerard We're going for chips.

Mrs Harte You are not.

Gerard Tara.

Mrs Harte Do you hear me?

Vincent Let's go down the park.

Gerard The gate'll be shut.

Vincent Let's go over the warmies.

Gerard Aw. No.

Vincent Let's go over the white-washed wall.

Gerard What for?

Vincent I don't know.

Gerard Let's go over the park.

Vincent Come on then. We'll climb over. Come on.

Gerard No. The parkie'll see us.

Vincent No he won't. We'll climb over.

Gerard I can't.

Vincent We'll squeeze through. You're skinny enough.

Gerard The afternoon was . . . it's evening anyway, almost very near. The afternoon . . . It was evening, it was evening. Late afternoon. Got out of bed. This is intolerable. And picked up a milk bottle. Stop. Went round the room collecting up milk bottles, pouring all the milk I found, into one. 'Ere that's gone off. Phew, I'm not surprised. There. Took a bottle of white medicine off the mantelpiece, uncorked it and took a swig. No. I put it back. There was nothing outside the window and

nothing when I opened the door. If I smoked I could be
lighting another cigarette, finger shaking, holding the
cigarette and a cup of coffee in the one hand. Laid my
head on the table. Don't go to sleep. Picked up my
trousers off the floor and put them on. There we are.
I wish I hadn't done that. I sat down and put my head
on the table again. Where was I? You're dying, talking,
experience hoarded is death. Thou shalt not take to
thyself any graven thing nor the likeness of anything
which is in the Heavens above or in the earth beneath.
Thou shalt not adore them nor serve them.

Mrs Harte I could lend you ten bob.

Gerard Thanks, that'll be fine.

Mrs Harte Now I want that back, remember?

Gerard Don't you always?

Mrs Harte You got me heart scalded. Why don't you
settle down? Job to job. What do you do up there
anyway?

Gerard What I do up there is I walk the streets.

Mrs Harte You'll come to grief.

Gerard I have quite literally.

Mrs Harte What have you got to be sorry for?

Gerard That's it.

Mrs Harte You ought to have my worries.

Gerard I do.

Mrs Harte I wish I could afford . . .

Gerard Money money money.

Mrs Harte You'll be the finish of me. You will.

Gerard You'll see to that, won't you?

Mrs Harte Honest to my God, isn't it terrible?

Gerard Sorry. Sorry. Sorry.

Mrs Harte If anyone's heart is broke it's mine.

Gerard Don't start.

Mrs Harte He was ill and I couldn't go up to him. Others went. I couldn't. I knew he wouldn't mind. No one expected me to by then, anyway. Then he died. Oh well.

Vincent Where is he?

Mrs Driscoll Who?

Vincent Him.

Mrs Driscoll I don't know.

Vincent Mmmm.

Mrs Driscoll Gone for a drink – don't ask me.

Vincent Where's my dinner?

Mrs Driscoll Sit down, don't panic, it'll be here.

Vincent I haven't got long.

Mrs Driscoll I know. I bet it's cold on the dock today.

Vincent It is.

Mrs Driscoll Did you see your father down there this morning?

Vincent Aye. Only for a second.

Mrs Driscoll I wonder when he'll be in.

Vincent (*yawning*) I don't know. That's what I said.

Mrs Driscoll What's the matter with you?

Vincent What do you mean?

Mrs Driscoll You've got 'em on you all of a sudden, haven't you? Come on, sit to the table. Haven't you got a fag?

Vincent No.

Mrs Driscoll What did you do with the five I bought you yesterday?

Vincent Smoked 'em, haven't I.

Mrs Driscoll Well, I don't know what a boy of your age wants smoking for any road.

Vincent No?

Mrs Driscoll What's up?

Vincent I don't know.

Mrs Driscoll There's something up.

Vincent No there isn't.

Mrs Driscoll If it's about finishing your time. You're finishing it, your time.

Vincent Well, I'm not finishing my time.

Mrs Driscoll You are finishing your time.

Vincent I'm not finishing my time.

Mrs Driscoll Vincent, don't, my nerves are bad this morning. You'll have to work your time. Don't be silly, Vincent.

Vincent Well, I'm not. I'm sick of not having any money. Aren't you? Don't you want any more money?

Mrs Driscoll Yes.

Vincent And I'm sick of having it thrown in my face.

Mrs Driscoll What?

Vincent Not bringing much money in. It's not my fault.

Mrs Driscoll Who said it was? What a thing to say. When did I throw it up at you, Vincent? What an awful thing to say.

Vincent Well?

Mrs Driscoll When?

Vincent Friday. Last Friday you did. Practically every Friday. Well, I'm packing it in. It's a big fiddle anyway.

Mrs Driscoll What is?

Vincent Down there. I know the trade. Well, I practically do. I can do as good a job as most fellas any road. Except for one or two of them.

Mrs Driscoll You don't know how lucky you are, that's your trouble. How many boys have got a trade? Tell me that.

Vincent How many wants one?

Mrs Driscoll Don't be silly.

Vincent It's bloody antique.

Mrs Driscoll What did you say?

Vincent It's antique. The yard is practically at a standstill. It's an antique system anyway, having to be put in for a trade. It's all a fiddle.

Mrs Driscoll How's it a fiddle?

Vincent What? It's not a fiddle, you keeping me on practically nothing for seven years, while they get free labour and skilled work, and then a skilled man at the end of it?

Mrs Driscoll Don't talk so stupid.

Vincent It's true.

Mrs Driscoll Well, if you want to look at it that way.

Vincent That's the only way to look at it.

Mrs Driscoll It's not the only way to look at it. I don't know. I don't see how it's a fiddle. It's a fair exchange to me. Look what your father would have done for a trade, but they were too poor and he had to bring in what he could.

Vincent I can get a job doing what I'm doing now.

Mrs Driscoll Don't be silly. They want skilled men.

Vincent I am a skilled man. I know the trade near as makes no difference.

Mrs Driscoll Don't be so big-headed, Vincent. It doesn't become you. You'll have to serve your time. You'll have to have signed indentures. I read it every night in the *Echo*. Only time-served men need apply.

Vincent Not for everything.

Mrs Driscoll You count yourself lucky.

Vincent Why should I?

Mrs Driscoll Why should you? Because you are. How many apprentices are there down the Mount Stuart? Go on, tell me. And how do you think you're one of them?

Vincent Oh, go on. That's right. Throw it up.

Mrs Driscoll Not through your father, that's for sure.

Vincent No, through yours. Go on.

Mrs Driscoll My father was a really skilled man and don't you forget it. Bloody Catholics.

Vincent What?

Mrs Driscoll Bloody Catholics with your religion and your Labour Party. You're all voice.

Vincent Better than no voice at all. It's a wonder you don't vote like him an' all. I don't think you think you should vote. You don't vote, do you?

Mrs Driscoll No. I don't see the point in women voting.

Vincent Nor me.

Mrs Driscoll I can't bear all this talk. I don't know anything and all I hear is talk. It wears me out.

Vincent I'm not just talking. I'm packing it in.

Mrs Driscoll Vincent, that's not doing anything.

Vincent Well, why don't you do something? Why don't you stand up to him? Why do you pick on me? You just want to be a slave, you do.

Mrs Driscoll I never wanted all this. I never came from all this.

Vincent What's wrong with it? This is nice. You keep it smashing, Mam.

Mrs Driscoll I don't want you down them yards. But what say do I have?

Vincent Why not? It's great down there. It is.

Mrs Driscoll Is it? I don't know. I don't know anything. Except I've heard of boys of fourteen running home because of the awful noise. But it's not for me to know. But I do know it's good to have a trade. You wanted to leave school.

Vincent I never did. You made me.

Mrs Driscoll We didn't. What good was another year's schooling going to do you, eh? You wanted to leave.

Vincent Well, I'm packing it in, all right?

Mrs Driscoll Stop it, Vincent, my nerves are awful bad.

Vincent You see, you always do that. Why can't you be on my side, Mam? You see. Aah. It's all right. Don't bother.

Mrs Driscoll He's grieving. I'd come if I could. He's grieving. He's never been a scrap of trouble to me, and I'd love to help him. I'd get out of this if I could. It's my fault I know. I'd come if I could.

Gerard The sun's blinding me.

Vincent Well, close your eyes then.

Gerard I'm testing them.

Vincent We ought to go in while the tide's up.

Gerard I'm too hot. Hey, is that a skylark?

Vincent Don't be soft, of course it isn't.

Gerard Well, what is it then? It's high enough up.

Vincent I don't know what it is. It's not a lark, that I do know.

Gerard How do you know?

Vincent Look, it's not a skylark.

Gerard Look, the moon's gone in.

Vincent Well?

Gerard I don't know what time it is. I'll get murdered.

Vincent Nor me. The pubs are out . . . listen . . . I'll get done.

Gerard And me. Look.

Vincent What?

Gerard Look up there.

Vincent What? What at?

Gerard Light has the fastest speed, right. Faster than sound.

Vincent Of course, it's faster than sound.

Gerard That's what I said. Look up there then. You looking?

Vincent Yeah.

Gerard I can't see you.

Vincent I'm looking.

Gerard I wish the moon would come out.

Vincent Why?

Gerard Now, take any star.

Vincent Is this a card trick?

Gerard No listen. Now a star, X distance from the earth is, when seen by us, Y times in its past. Right?

Vincent So what?

Gerard Do you agree?

Vincent Aye.

Gerard So that the world being X distance from the star would therefore from the star's point of view be Y times in its past. Do you agree?

Vincent Nah. Well, in the idea.

Gerard So if we were up there, we could be seeing, well, we, we'd be seeing anything. Something in the past, any road.

Vincent What?

Gerard Something. Depends. Something. Pyramids. Anything. Something. A man's life must be in existence for all time, this must be.

Vincent What for? What about time, though?

Gerard What?

Vincent Doesn't it have an end?

Gerard Dunno. I reckon not.

Vincent Anyway, that's all just an idea.

Gerard What do you mean, just an idea?

Vincent Well, I can't take it seriously.

Gerard Why not?

Vincent You can't prove it.

Gerard Of course you can prove it. I just have.

Vincent That's you, see. You want an easy solution, so it's all fixed. You can't prove an idea.

Gerard Of course you can. Of course you can prove an idea. What do you mean, you can't prove it?

Vincent Prove it then. I'd need evidence.

Gerard They could prove it.

Vincent How?

Gerard With a machine.

Vincent What machine?

Gerard I don't know. You're supposed to be good with your hands, you ought to be able to think of something.

Vincent Well, I can get the chain back on my bike without having a breakdown.

Gerard So can I get the chain back on my bike. I just can't mend a puncture. But I can get the chain back on my bike.

Vincent Not without having a nervous breakdown, you can't.

Gerard It's true enough, I bet, what I said.

Vincent It's just an idea. They'd need a machine. And if they did make a machine, you couldn't prove it.

Gerard Why not?

Vincent Because human life isn't long enough. You'd be dead before you got there.

Gerard Not if they got one to go fast enough. Got you.

Vincent Nah. They'll get to the moon though. You watch it. *Journey into Space.*

Gerard They won't, will they?

Vincent You don't like that, do you. What's the time then?

Gerard I don't know.

Vincent We'll get done. The moon's out again.

Gerard Look at it.

Vincent What?

Gerard The sun.

Vincent Why?

Gerard To test your eyes.

Vincent What, do you want me to go blind? You're up the wall, you are.

Gerard Isn't it hot? Coming in?

Vincent Nah. Don't you go in either.

Gerard Why not?

Vincent It is a lark and all. Two of them.

Gerard I'm going in.

Vincent The tide's on the turn. Look at it. You can't go in now.

Gerard I don't care.

Vincent Don't be daft, you know how fast it goes out.

Gerard I'm only going for a dip.

Vincent Don't be so bloody daft, Gerard.

Gerard I'm only going in for a dip.

Vincent No. Don't be so bloody daft, Gerard.

Mrs Driscoll Oh, Mrs Harte, I felt as if I didn't exist.
I kept looking out of the window and I couldn't work
out how it could be possible. It's easy to say so now,
because although I think it, I don't know it, if you can
take my meaning. And the line and the line-post and
everything. Well, the truth to tell I got very frightened,
so I locked the bedroom door and I lay on the bed. But I
couldn't stop my heart thumping. I was really frightened,
and I got so far down into myself I felt I should never
come back and I got into a real fright and I thought I
must work this off but I couldn't bear to have the baby
near me or to have to talk to our Colin so I slipped right
out of the back door. I got down the gully all right, but
when I came out on the main road I didn't know where
I was and this feeling, oh my God you wouldn't credit it.
I felt as if I was . . . Even now you're here and you're not
here. Isn't it dreadful? Oh, whatever am I going to do?

Mrs Harte It's not as if we've got a bit of brandy. It's
terrible to be poor.

Mrs Driscoll Oh Jesus . . . Oh dear. (*She laughs.*) In
the street Mr Riley took my arm and I felt a bit better.
He's such a gentleman. Do you ever get this feeling? It's
awful. It's happening, but how can it be happening? Like
I feel as if I'm not here. I feel as if I don't exist at all.
How can I exist? Now I'm just saying that. That's what
I felt like. I can't go on like this. I'm not going to shout,
but it won't go away.

Mrs Harte Come on, love.

Mrs Driscoll Go away.

Mrs Harte Come on.

Mrs Driscoll No.

Mrs Harte Yes, come on, come on, come on, my love.

Mrs Driscoll Don't make it worse. I'll settle down. Don't worry about me. Oh, oh. I'll have to go back. I can't stand still.

Mrs Harte You just try.

Mrs Driscoll Thank you.

Mrs Harte Dear, dear, dear. You stay in here. Gerard'll pop in next door and see everything is all right. You come and lie in here, my love.

Mrs Driscoll I'm awfully sorry.

Vincent Is my mother in here?

Mrs Driscoll Yes. I won't be long. Go on. Isn't it terrible. Vincent!

Mrs Harte Hello, Vincent.

Mrs Driscoll Go on. I'll be in in a minute.

Vincent They want their tea.

Mrs Driscoll It's all ready. I'll be in in a minute.

Mrs Harte Go on, son. She'll be in.

Vincent Michael's crying.

Mrs Driscoll I know, I can hear him, can't I?

Vincent Look, Eileen's got to go out.

Mrs Driscoll Go in, go in, will you?

Mrs Harte Go on, son.

Vincent Why doesn't she come in?

Mrs Harte She'll be in.

Vincent Our dad's in.

Mrs Driscoll He's not, is he?

Vincent No, he isn't.

Mrs Driscoll What did you say that for?

Vincent Because he will be in. He should be in.

Mrs Driscoll Vincent. Vincent! Vincent! (*screaming*) Come here! Oh dear, oh dear, oh dear.

Mrs Harte She was a strange girl. Poor girl. And him, he's as ignorant as they come. Like your grandfather Harte. Bloody Bible-punching old get. Your grandmother wanted her hair cut when we all did because she used to get so hot in that kitchen with that big range. He wouldn't allow it. He said a woman's hair is her crowning glory, as if the bloody Bible said what length. Ignorant old bigot. I'd have cleaved him open. Bloody Bible-punching old get. Like him next door, and he's nothing to write home about. She says she can't find no love in her for her kids and yet look how she keeps them. I wish I had a quarter of her energy. And she sends him to church and to a Catholic school. She's a damn sight better than half of them that go. She's a strange girl. She comes from a lovely family. You should see her sister's home. *She*'s a smart woman. And he's years older than her. I don't know whatever she saw in him. I can't bear him. Heavy, big, dark thing he is.

Gerard Rattling through my dry mind like peas or lentils or rice blown through my fingers, across the pane and across my eyes the grasses' tops are thrown. The fields are nervous, their contents quivering. Field after field after field, all shaking with nerves. I'm exhausted looking out of train windows. I'd like to jump out of here at this speed, and retain this speed's magic freedom, unhampered by the moquette seating and that cream-and-green ceiling and grubby walls and those pictures of the pump room Llandrindod Wells and pictures of Burnham-on-Sea, and fly out on a kite string, and describe in the air currents and shapes, determined by the train's speed, going and never arriving, and feel the occasional tough jerk at the end of my tether, reminding me of restrictions, but feeling its immediate release, billowing me out to freedom and safety and purpose.

Mrs Harte I wish I could come up when you're ill like that. What did you get ill like that for? I nearly died with worry – you up there and I can't get up to you. How are you?

Gerard Oh, much better.

Mrs Harte Are you feeling any better?

Gerard Oh, much.

Mrs Harte You had me worried to death. How did you get ill like that? What were you doing?

Gerard Nothing.

Mrs Harte You must have done something to get ill like that.

Gerard Nothing.

Mrs Harte You ought to have stopped in the army that time. That's what you ought to have done. You had a good career ahead of you there. You gave up an easy billet there.

Gerard Literally.

Mrs Harte In the Far East. It would have killed me.
You're drifting away from me. I feel a dead failure . . .
I wish I could come up when you're ill like that. Are you
feeling better?

Gerard Much.

Mrs Harte If anything happened to you, I'd lose my
mind. When you ran away I was so frightened.

Gerard What do you mean, ran away? I never ran away.

Mrs Harte You just slammed out of the house. Now
I think you've run away for good, haven't you?

Gerard I'm here, aren't I?

Mrs Harte But you're drifting away from me.

Gerard I can't stay here. I hate it.

Mrs Harte Not as much as me, I can tell you.

Gerard Come back with me.

Mrs Harte I wouldn't fit in up there.

Gerard Come back with me. I'll find a place.

Mrs Harte I'd love it, but it's not to be.

Gerard Why?

Mrs Harte Don't ask me, son. That's how it is. I wish
I could cry like that.

Gerard Silly, isn't it?

Mrs Harte Yes.

Gerard Come with me, please. Oh please. Let's run
away together. You and me. For Christ's sake don't cry,
Mam, it will kill me.

Mrs Harte I don't cry.

Gerard Oh Jesus, you're crying.

Mrs Harte I'm not crying.

Gerard I am.

Mrs Harte I'm not.

Gerard Nor am I, now.

Mrs Harte I never cry.

Gerard I don't much. Never.

Mrs Harte You always used to cry.

Gerard You don't cry.

Mrs Harte No. Leave that to everyone else, I'm sorry I couldn't come up to see you. But you must know me by now. Too much of a coward.

Gerard I didn't expect it.

Mrs Harte What do you mean?

Gerard That I didn't expect you to come up.

Mrs Harte What's that supposed to mean?

Gerard What I said.

Mrs Harte You can be cruel sometimes.

Gerard Can I?

Mrs Harte When you going back?

Gerard I don't know.

Mrs Harte I expect I'll see you sooner than I think I will.

Gerard The trees closed like fir-cones as the train sped under them and they receded. The sun made a hot ring in the clouds, like its reflection through a magnifying glass on the back of your hand or on paper you want to burn. The train went through the countryside as if it would break the weather. Smoke from a fire stained the air above a whole field. It began to get cooler and look greener. There were dark patches in the fields. It was as if huge animals had been sleeping in them.

Mrs Harte I couldn't get you out of my sight at one time, now I think you've run away for good.

Gerard What say?

Mrs Harte You're drifting away from me.

Gerard I'm here, aren't I?

Mrs Harte But you're drifting away from me.

Gerard I can't stop here, I hate it.

Mrs Harte Not as much as me, I can tell you.

Gerard Let's blow it up.

Mrs Harte Come here. Keep still. You're going grey.

Gerard What you . . . Don't!

Mrs Harte How old are you? Keep still. When I was your age I had three or four kids.

Gerard Come back with me.

Mrs Harte I wouldn't fit in up there.

Gerard Come back with me. I'll find a place.

Mrs Harte I'd love it but it's not to be.

Gerard Why not, why not?

Mrs Harte Why? Don't ask me, son. That's how it is.
I wish I could cry like that.

Gerard I'm all right, I'm tired of the train. Silly, isn't it?

Mrs Harte It is.

Gerard Come back with me, please. Let's run away
together, you and me.

Mrs Harte Don't talk so soft.

Gerard I'll never give you up.

Mrs Harte What?

Gerard I'd be afraid to.

Mrs Harte You might have to.

Gerard No have to. I can order experience in my nut
if I want to.

Mrs Harte You'll soon get snapped up. Come here.
You're going grey. I had two or three children when
I was your age.

Gerard I'll never give you up.

Mrs Harte Don't talk so soft. You'll get snapped up.

Gerard I'd be afraid to.

Mrs Harte You might have to.

Mrs Harte I watched it. I would have helped had it
been possible. I would have stopped had I known in
time. Had one known one would have, don't you think?
I wouldn't have wanted it, would I? But I watched from
a good seat going through much the same myself.

Mrs Harte When you ran away.

Gerard What?

Mrs Harte You ran away.

Gerard I didn't run away.

Mrs Harte For hours it seemed.

Gerard I'll run away from you.

Mrs Harte What?

Gerard You said it often enough.

Mrs Harte I should have done, that's what I should have done, run away from all of you.

Gerard I'd like to run away from all of you.

Mrs Harte What?

Gerard That's what you said.

Mrs Harte When you ran away I was so frightened.

Gerard Don't bring all that up. I only went over the tide.

Mrs Harte You slammed out of the house.

Gerard I walked over the tide, I forgot.

Mrs Harte For hours it seemed.

Gerard I never said I'd run away.

Mrs Harte I thought you meant it.

Gerard I never said I'd run away.

Mrs Harte You did.

Gerard It was you.

Mrs Harte Now you've run away for good.

Gerard Mam.

Mrs Harte Yet there was a time I couldn't move without you round me grizzling.

Gerard When I first come back . . .

Mrs Harte What are you saying?

Gerard When you were first ill I needn't have come back.

Mrs Harte What?

Gerard I wasn't writing.

Mrs Harte You didn't write much.

Gerard That's what I said.

Mrs Harte You came back quick enough when it suited you. You'd better go back, I think.

Gerard I wish I hadn't come back, I can tell you. I wish I hadn't left to come back, I wish I hadn't been here to have to come back, I can tell you.

Mrs Harte Oh, that's nice. You needn't come back. On your way, brother. Pack your bags, mate. What do you think I've got to keep you on?

Gerard What are you talking about? What are you talking about?

Mrs Harte You'll be the finish of me, you will.

Gerard You'll see to that, won't you?

Mrs Harte You're a bully and you always have been a bully. What did you come back for? Go away. Leave me alone. What have you come back for?

Gerard Because you're the only thing I have to show off with. You're the only thing that contents me. You're the only thing I have. That's all I have. It's all I have. You're all I have.

Mrs Harte If anyone's heart's broke, it's mine. And to think there was a time I couldn't go to the toilet without you banging on the door.

Gerard She doesn't exist. Not so long as she's in here. But she's pushing her way out as her fear becomes my hysterical talk. She pushes her way out so I clench my teeth. She pushes against them. Eases through them and I can't close them. They're aching.

Gerard Look out the back. Look out the back.

Mrs Harte What?

Gerard Look at it. Why don't you clear it up? Why don't you? Why don't you?

Mrs Harte Why should I?

Gerard Why shouldn't you?

Mrs Harte God give me patience.

Gerard Why?

Mrs Harte I'm sick of it. I'm sick of it. I'm sick of it.

Vincent Mrs Harte?

Mrs Harte Who's that?

Vincent It's me.

Mrs Harte Who's that?

Vincent It's me, Mrs Harte.

Mrs Harte Vincent. Come in, Vincent. What is it?
Gerard's out. I don't know where he is. I haven't been in
long myself. Haven't you seen him?

Vincent No.

Mrs Harte He won't be long. At least he shouldn't be
long. You wait till he *does* come in. Sit down, son.

Vincent No, thanks.

Mrs Harte And if you're going out, the pair of you, be
in a bit earlier. Sit down, Vincent. He won't be long.

Vincent Do you think you could . . .

Mrs Harte What, love?

Vincent I think the door's stuck. I can't get no answer.

Mrs Harte Where is she?

Vincent The door's stuck. I can't get no answer.

Mrs Harte Where is she? Vincent. Vincent!

Vincent She's in the . . .

Mrs Harte Vincent.

Vincent She's in the . . .

Mrs Harte Where?

Vincent In the . . .

Mrs Harte When I did go in, I called and called. Then
I got the oldest girl to take the other children down their
aunt's. I kept the baby with me. Where is she? What is it?
Where is she?

Vincent She's in the . . .

Mrs Harte I'll go in. You stay here. Gerard won't be long. When I did go in, I tried the door, but I couldn't get it to budge. So I had to get a hammer to it. Mrs Driscoll!

Gerard He-llo! You in here?

Vincent Yeah.

Gerard Where's my mother? Is she in yet? I'll get murdered. I said I'd come straight home. Where is she? What's the matter?

Mrs Harte Mrs Driscoll.

Gerard What's the matter?

Mrs Harte I couldn't get the door to budge. I tried forcing it. But I couldn't get it to budge. So I had to get a hammer to it. Mrs Driscoll! Sheila!

Gerard Your mother's having a baby, I think.

Vincent She is not.

Gerard She is.

Vincent She is not. How would you know?

Gerard My mother told me.

Vincent She did not. She is not.

Gerard She is. I heard her tell my mother.

Mrs Harte She wasn't a great deal younger than me . . . silly girl. Oh, she was a nice girl. A really nice girl. She didn't look any different, except for the burns on the side of her mouth.

Gerard You coming out after?

Vincent No.

Mrs Harte Come on now, Mrs Driscoll, love. Mrs Driscoll. Can you hear me, dear? Perhaps if I'd been in earlier? No.

Gerard Aw, come on.

Vincent Shut up, you.

Mrs Harte So I had to get a hammer to it. But I couldn't find one.

Gerard What's the matter?

Vincent Oh, shut up, you.

Mrs Harte Where's the hammer, Gerard?

Gerard I don't know. What d'you want a hammer for?

Mrs Harte Where the hell is it? Where's your father?

Vincent He's still in work, I think.

Mrs Harte Where's your father?

Gerard I don't know.

Mrs Harte Go on out, the two of you. Go on. Go on out. Out.

Vincent Mam.

Gerard What's the matter?

Mrs Harte It doesn't matter.

Gerard What's the matter?

Mrs Harte Be quiet, you. Where the hell is it?

Vincent Let us in, Mam.

Gerard What is it, Mam?

Vincent Mam.

Gerard Mam?

Mrs Harte What?

Gerard Don't go in there.

Mrs Harte Why not?

Gerard I don't like her.

Vincent Mammy!

Mrs Harte What do you mean?

Vincent I can't get no answer.

Mrs Harte Gerard. Run down the Presbytery. Damn it all. Go on. The both of you. Go on. Mrs Driscoll! Mrs Driscoll! The oldest girl went to live away. He kept the others except for the baby, who went down the auntie's. The oldest boy went to sea. I got splinters in my arm breaking down the door. I brought the baby in with me. I'll bring the baby in here, Vincent. I've sent Eileen down your auntie's, love.

Gerard What's the matter?

Vincent Eileen went to live away. *He* kept the others except for the baby, who went down my auntie's. I went to sea. I see him shuffling round. I got a place when I come home and got them all together. They're all married now. I see their kids. I suppose you think an injustice has been done. To him, I mean, he still works. No he doesn't. He's given it up now. I can't fathom out when she exactly decided it. She give me a note for the chemist. For some cleaning stuff. He wouldn't give it to me. Then he did. Poor bloke.

Mrs Harte Then he went to sea, I think. I don't know whether it was the Merchant or the Royal.

Gerard It was the Merchant. It was the Merchant.

Mrs Harte Poor man.

Gerard Who?

Mrs Harte Him next door. He was all right. He was a quiet enough bloke.

Vincent He was about nine and he was dancing about.

Mrs Harte I brought the baby in with me.

Vincent Coming out, Ger?

Gerard I can't, she won't let me.

Mrs Harte Then he died.

Vincent I was cold.

Mrs Harte Oh well.

Vincent So I went indoors.

Mrs Harte He was a lovely boy. He was lost at sea.

Gerard In the other photograph are other children. None of them is me.

Mrs Harte I scraped all my hand. I got splinters all up my arm.

Gerard Look at the sky.

Vincent Dear Daddy, I hope you are well, that you are in good health and that it's all right where you are. Dear Daddy, I wish you were home. Dear Daddy, I wish you could come home for good. I hope I'll get another postcard again. We all got our cards and we hope you got ours. Lots of love, your son till death – John Vincent O'Driscoll.

Two

Gerard He was sitting opposite me. I look like my mother in every way except for the hair, he said. It was New Year's Eve. We smuggled two bottles of whiskey into the squadron cinema with us. We'd already finished the other bottle. Or rather he had, really. I was attached to a Scots regiment and it was New Year's Eve. We drank from the neck, turn and turn about and then out of bravado he opened his mouth wide and poured nearly half a bottle down his throat and then he pulled my head back and tried to pour some down mine. I laughed and choked and giggled. We slumped back, our knees up against the heads in front, knees against our heads, heads on shoulders and shoulders supporting heads. We watched the film shouting and drunk. We'd all seen it before. Once that week. We were soaked with sweat. The two fans in the tin roof didn't make a blind bit of difference.

Vincent It was very cold. He could have only been about nine. I could have watched him for hours, dancing about. I chuckled, he was so comical. He was having the time of his life. But it was cold. So I went back in by the fire. I was in digs at the time. Down Grange, I think.

Gerard We were shouting, greeting people, yelling Happy New Year to people as we made our way down the main road. Who shouted and greeted us. Groups and pairs singing and shouting, arms around each other. Fighting. Two squaddies fighting quite viciously, slogging away covered in dust. We wandered under the verandahs of the officers' quarters, and saw one or two poor bastards trying to sleep in their rooms, turning under their nets.

164

Humourless bastards. We walked along the broken floors of the abandoned section near the boundary. Empty rooms. Mesh doors banging. Sand filling some of the rooms almost up to the ceiling. We sat down. He sat opposite me. You've got hair just like my mother, he said. Grabbing. Where did you get it? I told him. Oh Jesus, he said. So we lay on the steps for hours, half-talking, half-singing, half-sleeping.

Vincent She left cupboards and cupboards of clothes. Silk blouses and silk dresses. Hangers of them. And drawers of underclothes and stockings. Pale silk underwear and silk stockings with seams. And shoes and bags and scarfs. And handkerchiefs tucked away in drawers . . . And we found shoe boxes full of letters, love letters, and our birthday cards and a locket with hair in it and a little white baby shoe even, and old old cards. Couldn't have been hers, with lace edges. And the stink of scent and powder. We had to live with it months after her.

Gerard She left jewellery mostly. Rubbish really, but very pretty. Trinkets really, but some quite nice pieces as well. A crystal cross I liked. Nothing very much. A clip I liked and her rings and of course her books and drawings. No money of course. Very little. Well, hardly any really.

Prolonged laughter from Vincent and Gerard.

Vincent We practically had the nine o'clock run.

Gerard Did you . . .

Vincent Do you . . .

Gerard Was it . . . Were you . . . Did we . . .

Vincent When you . . . When I . . .

Gerard Were you . . . Did you . . . (*He opens his mouth to speak again but can't.*)

Vincent Speak up.

Mrs Harte I got your magazine. The flowers I gave to one of the women who was very ill to cheer her up. The other woman and myself had a room to ourselves in the convalescent home. You'd think we were staying in the Ritz. You've no need to come home, you know. You don't look well. Don't think too harsh of me, will you? You saved my reason. Nobody don't know nothing about all that money. Don't say anything will you? Is that why you've come back?

Gerard Of course it isn't.

Mrs Harte Oh come back. I'll look after you. Don't cry. I haven't been out since last week, so that's cheerful. I haven't seen anybody. Ah, you're the best of the bunch. I'd sooner put paid to myself than ask anything of any of them. Don't be unhappy. You've been no disappointment, not even a worry really. You're a good boy. Don't be unhappy. I may have been wrong and no doubt I'll have to pay for it . . . but don't be unhappy.

Gerard Where are they? You've been taking sleeping tablets during the day.

Mrs Harte I haven't.

Gerard You have. Look at you. Listen, you've got to change. You've got to. You're killing me. You've got to stop.

Mrs Harte I've only had a bottle of Guinness.

Gerard I know. I can smell. You can hardly stand up. You've got to change.

Mrs Harte Don't be silly. I'll be all right.

Gerard You've got to change. Damn it all, you've got to stop. You've got to leave me alone.

Mrs Harte Don't.

Gerard You must. Listen to me. You've got to. Are you listening, Mam?

Mrs Harte I'm listening.

Gerard You've got to. Why don't you stop?

Mrs Harte Don't be foolish. Now leave me alone.

Gerard What's the matter with you, eh?

Mrs Harte Nothing.

Gerard What's the matter with you, eh? What is it you want? Come on, what is it? What do you want, Mam?

Mrs Harte I'm paying dear for any wrong I did in the past.

Gerard What is it? What is it you want? What do you want?

Mrs Harte There isn't anything I want, only peace of mind.

Gerard Oh . . .

Mrs Harte Ssh . . . Listen.

Gerard What to?

Mrs Harte Sh. Sh. There's the train. Whenever I hear a train I want to be on it. I don't know what we moved for. I never liked it here. I had lovely neighbours. Lovely folk-weave curtains. I miss that back-to-back grate.

Gerard I was ashamed of you. Utterly. Of myself. Utterly.

Mrs Harte Are you any better?

Gerard Of course.

Mrs Harte I wish I could come up when you're like that.

Gerard No, of course not, of course not. Of course not. I've been desperately trying to die ever since you, I don't know the date. When was it? Ever since you decided it. I've hundreds of letters from you. They're all about nothing but you haven't any money. Money. Money. Money. Money. Money. Money. Money. Money. Money. Can't you manage?

Mrs Harte No, I can't manage, anything.

Gerard You can't manage anything. You've got to stop. You've got to become who you're supposed to be, who you told me you were, they told me you were, you believed you were. I know who you are. It's not good enough. I've become what? An imitation of what you're not actually yourself. You had better die. There's got to be a moment. Do you remember it? I saw you decide it was all up for you, I observed, eating the side of that cream-and-green pram. Do you? Do you, eh? You had better die.

Mrs Harte I don't want to die! I want to take part. I don't want to be one of those old crows who've grown old gracefully and go with dignity when their time comes because they can't bear what's going on because they know they've got no control of it. I'm afraid to die. I must be hard. I don't think so.

Mrs Driscoll How are you then?

Mrs Harte I'm fine. I've got the kettle on. Thank Christ for a sit down.

Mrs Driscoll The baby's out the front asleep. Michael's took himself down our Julie's.

Mrs Harte And mine are out till dinner time. Let's sit down for Christ's sake. Thank God for those back-to-back grates.

Mrs Driscoll I'd say.

Mrs Harte I've got the kettle on it. It saves me a lot in coppers. I thought I heard Vincent.

Mrs Driscoll Yes. He's gone down the shop for me. He's been home since last Wednesday week. He'd a kick playing football and he forgot to go back.

Mrs Harte So that's cheerful.

Mrs Driscoll He's got me heart scalded. I told him to stay in school. But no. And now he don't want to finish his time.

Mrs Harte Well, it won't be worth the time he has spent.

Mrs Driscoll You try telling him that. I've been up since six.

Mrs Harte What for?

Mrs Driscoll I don't know. I've been working.

Mrs Harte You're better today. You look better.

Mrs Driscoll I am. I feel better.

Mrs Harte *He's* got a cold and is happy as ever can be.

Mrs Driscoll I brought the paper back.

Mrs Harte Thanks.

Mrs Driscoll I see Churchill's gone on holiday.

Mrs Harte Yerra, he's been on holiday all his life, that fella. Bloody warmongering bloody old get. Bloody cigar. I hate low men.

Mrs Driscoll I see they've painted Nye for Prye on the bridge.

Mrs Harte Oh him, bloody Communist bloody get. Ah well.

She sighs. Mrs Driscoll begins to sing. Sweetly.

I haven't heard that for years.

She whistles and joins in with phrases she knows.

Come on.

Mrs Driscoll What?

Mrs Harte Up you get.

Mrs Driscoll I can't lead.

Mrs Harte Nor can I. Hang on. Here we are.

They dance. Very well. Singing and talking.

What is it?

Mrs Driscoll I don't know.

Mrs Harte My Christ, when did you last have a dance?

Mrs Driscoll I don't know.

They laugh.

Look out there.

Mrs Harte What?

Mrs Driscoll That old fella up the top. He can't believe his eyes. We'd better stop.

Mrs Harte What for? Let him look.

They dance on until Mrs Harte stops.

Christ. There's the door. It's the club man.

Mrs Driscoll Well, he knows I'm in. The baby's out the front.

Mrs Harte Well, you're not there. You're in here. Come on out the back door and into Mrs Wallis's before he twigs. She's got different callers.

Mrs Driscoll Just my luck if Vincent is coming up the street.

Mrs Harte If Gerard comes out of school early, I'll blind him.

Gerard I'm exhausted looking out of train windows. No sense but sight, no touch or scent, so that one can't smell or feel. Silent as film dissolves. Better the train's smell, the train's noise, the city view, the townsman's countryside. Pan is locked up in this train and panic. No apocalyptic vision of the nineteenth century. No smashing through the sunshine past redbrick mills and factories like cathedrals. Last glimpses, all like last glimpses. A need to feed and record. The need, but no accurate recording apparatus. It's like eating without chewing. Last glimpses. Broken stone, broken pram, broken tractor, broken lorry, broken wood, broken iron, broken car, broken bike, broken water, broken tiles. A boy in red. Boys' arms around each other. Council, fields, houses, paint on walls, broken sentences, broken chair. Pulped cars, mashed, piled high, like pulped metal paper, giving nothing to the future. Skirt cities. Outside they leave behind things to grow over with seeds of the country. They've run to seed. Old train terminuses with broken platforms. Like being on a ghost train this. Lovely as graveyards can be, ones that they're going to knock down and run roads over, as ones that are going to be run over by cars, hundreds of cars. Buildings are overgrown like the countryside itself is overgrown. Domesticated, turning them into follies. Don't kill the chance of beauty. This beauty. Collected like junk in the country's attic. They have their meaning, I'm sure. On we zip, the ghost train through other stations and halts. Then the red starts. Dark, dark red. The berries are huge, there was no frost in the spring. Birds are the only wildlife in this countryside. One magpie. Two for joy. So much red it seems like an obsession, so, observe. It's not an obsession. Obsessive about what is there. So many berries and bushes, the greens and reds mixing, each losing its intensity, defocused, mixed so to speak, defocused, confused by their intensity and this speed. Thick with berries like ampoules of oil. The reddening reminds me of harsh winter afternoons with willows reddening in the spring. Red September. Hydrangeas soaked in red. Some trees starting to gleam, glowing, passing, fail and then glow. Single trees like these are creating aureoles in woods. Llanwern turning red with dust. Miles of blue laminated boxes under red dust. The green between the two towns has hedges, they're red. Red pullovers on lovers with a dog, one red arm round another red shoulder. The reens are covered still in their slime. Pulling in, past the old town, the Dowlais, the old works is chalked in red madder on a blue ground. Hiding in the smoke but not lost to view. Arrived in Argos, experience the bus service and all the impelled feelings are disgruntled and litter-ridden.

Vincent What, you home then for a couple of days like, I suppose?

Gerard Aye. That's right.

Vincent I've come over here for a pint. Where you going?

Gerard Nowhere.

Vincent When you going back?

Gerard Monday, I suppose. I don't know. I don't have to go back Monday . . . I don't know when I'm going back.

Vincent Aren't you working?

Gerard Yes.

Vincent Do you fancy a drink?

Gerard No thanks.

Vincent It's not a bad pint over here. I'd rather have a pint in a pub though, any day of the week. I don't like clubs. Though it's not a bad pint over here.

Gerard It's too full of people for me. People I can't hardly remember or people who can't remember me, or people I don't know who keep on talking to me, or people I do know, but whose names I've forgotten, or people I don't want to know anyway. It gets too crowded for me.

Vincent I sit quiet, me. Down the other end. Mmm?

Gerard No thanks, I'm not drinking.

Vincent OK. All my *old* haunts have been ruined or pulled down.

Gerard In town?

Vincent Yeah. Or been pulled down. I used to drink in the North and South. That's been pulled down. The Packet's been ruined, the Gun's full of students. I used to drink a lot in the Tredegar one time.

Gerard Oh aye.

Vincent That's been pulled down.

Gerard It isn't, I passed it on my way home.

Vincent No, the Tredegar up Bute Terrace.

Gerard Oh aye, I saw they'd closed it down.

Vincent Yeah. You can't get a decent pint anywhere.

Gerard You sound like an old man.

Vincent Yeah. Sometimes when I'm waiting for the bus, I think, Christ, I'm getting like all the old men up the station running to catch their last bus home to Christ knows what hole.

Gerard Do you know, I imagined you were still at sea.

Vincent What? No fear.

Gerard Didn't you like it then?

Vincent I haven't been to sea for years.

Gerard Don't you miss it, then?

Vincent I don't know. You seeing your old man?

Gerard Yeah.

Vincent I haven't been to sea for years.

Gerard Ay, do you remember Mrs Dwyer?

Vincent Who?

Gerard You know.

Vincent I don't know.

Gerard You do know.

Vincent I don't.

Gerard You do.

Vincent The woman with her hair in pipe-cleaners?

Gerard Yeah.

Vincent Blimey.

Gerard She still has her hair in pipe-cleaners.

Vincent Does she still like a drink?

Gerard I don't know. Anyway I saw her the other day. She had her arm in a sling.

Vincent She still likes a drink, then.

Gerard No, that's it. I said, How do you do that, Mrs Dwyer?

Vincent What did she say then?

Gerard She said, You wouldn't mind if you did it drunk, she said. But I got it falling out of church.

Vincent Oh aye.

Gerard How do you fall out of church?

Vincent Same way as she falls out of the Moorland. Blimey, she must be getting on.

Gerard Aye. Ey, Mrs De-wyer. Cun we 'av ou' borl back?

Vincent I got chucked off the altar because of you.

Gerard I got chucked off the altar because of you, you mean.

Vincent That was after you got me chucked off. How long you been home, then?

Gerard Why? A fortnight. I should have gone back last week, I suppose. I'll go back on Monday. Though I don't have to go back. I don't know when I'll go back.

Vincent How's your old man?

Gerard Don't you think about it at all?

Vincent What, going to sea? Nah.

Gerard Don't you miss it?

Vincent How is he? Funny thing, I saw my old man not so long back.

Gerard Oh yeah.

Vincent Oh, my old man was great, you know. He was. We had some great times. I remember us going out once. Or even twice. No. Fair enough. He worked hard.

Gerard He worked on the dock, didn't he?

Vincent He did. He was a scruffer.

Gerard What's a scruffer?

Vincent Well might you ask.

Gerard What?

Vincent What a scruffer is.

Gerard What is a scruffer?

Vincent He shacked up with some blonde piece. In fact he's still with her. Poor old bugger. I can't blame him. He's stuck with her. Or she's stuck with him. He give her the runaround for years. First one and then the other. He must be donkey-rigged, like me. Ha. I saw them the other week. He didn't see me. He was half boozed. And her. She was stuttered, she was. You should have seen her face, blimey. And her hair. To match. He was walking ahead of her.

Gerard Where was this then?

Vincent In town.

Gerard I was in town.

Vincent Today? Did you get caught in the rain?

Gerard When?

Vincent Earlier on.

Gerard No, was it raining? I must have been home by then.

Vincent It bucketed down.

Gerard Were you in town?

Vincent Yeah, I was flying, me. I rushed into the Wyndham Arcade. Then I got a lift off of a mate of mine.

Gerard So you were all right.

Vincent I should say. Barney Williams. You don't know him.

Gerard You wanna watch you don't catch a chill.

Vincent Aye.

Gerard Yeah.

Vincent I'm surprised you didn't catch it over here. It must have been just in town. Don't you fancy a drink?

Gerard No thanks.

Vincent I can't hardly believe I was at sea at all sometimes. I must have enjoyed it too much. Are you sure?

Gerard Positive. Honest.

Vincent Do you know the only proof I've got is the tattoos on my arms.

Gerard On your arms?

Vincent Yeah.

Gerard You'll get murdered.

Vincent Only on my arms.

Gerard I went with a Scotch bloke once to get tattooed. Thank God I changed my mind. He didn't. What's it say?

Vincent Mum.

Gerard Mum!

Vincent Yeah. A crowd of us went after a piss-up. In the Mediterranean somewhere. The Canal I suppose. I tell a lie. It must have been. Or was it, it must have been. They say you get tattooed three times. First your mother, then your girl, then your wife. I just got the two.

Gerard Who's the other?

Vincent Jan. And I haven't seen her for two years. Took the baby and fucked off. Mind you, I can't be much to live with. Let's go for a drink. Coming for a drink?

Gerard No.

Vincent She always wanted to go out. Skittles. The club. The fruit machine. Or talk. I couldn't talk. *She* couldn't talk. Just a stream of the most effing stupid things she'd picked up. And I'm no bloody good with my hands. Well, I could be I suppose. I used to be. But I got no application. I'm not working a seven-day week and then coming home making fitted fucking cupboards. She had lovely dark hair but she dyed it black all the time. So it was sticky. She had . . . She . . . I can't be bothered now. They hang about me sometimes. I'd sooner use the pros up Bute Terrace if I'm pushed. Outside the Key Beck. Then there was the fuss about him being brought up a Catholic and all that. As if *I* cared. Particularly after the fuss over my mother's funeral. She agreed. She should have stuck by it. I can't think why I made such a fuss now – it doesn't make a blind bit of difference to me. Don't you fancy one?

Gerard No, honest.

Vincent Sometimes I'll catch sight of a woman and there's that look. That, that . . .

Gerard I look away.

Vincent Sometimes I'll want to give up my seat on a bus. But I can't. Like I saw this young girl. She only looked about sixteen. All made up to bring you down. But she was so tired. So tired. She was holding one kid and she was pregnant, and she had another by the hand, but I don't think it was hers. But I couldn't stand up. I don't know how to anyway. I look out of the window. It's their fucking faces. You want to knock their fucking faces in for looking like that. They filled the East Dock in.

Gerard I wonder if we were in there.

Vincent Oh come for a drink, Ger.

Gerard No.

Vincent Come on.

Gerard I said no.

Vincent You did for me, you know.

Mrs Driscoll Vincent.

Gerard What?

Vincent You did, you know.

Gerard I did for you?

Mrs Driscoll Vincent.

Gerard *I*. *I* did for you? *I* did?

Mrs Harte Gerard.

Gerard *I* did for you?

Mrs Harte Gerard.

Gerard *I* did?

Mrs Harte Gerard.

Vincent You did, you know.

Mrs Driscoll Vincent.

Gerard *I* did?

Mrs Harte Gerard.

Mrs Driscoll Mrs Harte, Mrs Harte.

Mrs Harte I'm sick of it. I'm sick of it. I'm sick of it.

Vincent I'm going in.

Gerard Don't go in.

Mrs Driscoll Oh, I'm terrified. Jesus, I'm terrified.

Vincent I'll have to.

Mrs Harte I'll split you.

Gerard Go on in then.

Mrs Driscoll Oh dear, oh dear.

Vincent Don't worry, I am.

Mrs Harte I'll cleave you. I'll tear you.

Vincent You did, you know.

Mrs Driscoll Mrs Harte.

Gerard *I* did.

Mrs Harte Oh, I'm fed up.

Vincent He was only about nine and he was dancing about.

Gerard I know.

Vincent I was cold.

Gerard You must have been.

Vincent How do you know?

Mrs Harte I'm bleeding.

Vincent How do you know?

Mrs Harte Oh, I'm bleeding.

Gerard In my hospital pain draws attention to the terminal case . . . All day he's fluttered his arms, let his blackened arms drift in the air. His wife's face is like a cyst. She tries to rest her head against him. He growls like a comic. Her glasses are knocked to the floor. Oh, I don't know what he means.

Mrs Driscoll I think it's inclined to rain.

Gerard The three lamps in the ceiling are burning with dry ice. The sun is hanging underneath the old man's bed. The three white lamps are the three moons of the ward. The ward is tropical now and full of difficult beasts. The white globes flood red for night and we can't sleep.

Vincent It's no use. It's no use.

Gerard In her hospital ward. The sadism of a hospital death. Making the dying cough up their lives.

Vincent So I had to borrow a suitcase.

Gerard I walked along the corridors to pass the time. Up the stairs to the doctors' common rooms and found the notice board and on it the next day's list. Her name typed on it. You can never be sure you exist in their minds really. It's odd to find you must exist after all. It's so real, the pain, you don't exist. And then on the other hand, the pain, you do exist.

Vincent It was too.

Gerard Arms above her head. Beyond lowering her eyelids. Aboriginal. Girl's head. Wooden mouth. Burnt sienna eyelids. I'm going to be sick. Are you?

Vincent I must. I must.

Mrs Harte Oh, I'm fed up.

Gerard I shall never break faith with her. I'll never give her up.

Mrs Harte Oh, I'm fed up.

Vincent I should have. I should have.

Mrs Driscoll Oh, much better.

Gerard What you don't realise is that the death of someone who has been wronged can never be avenged on anyone.

Vincent He was only about nine, the poor little fella. I was cold.

Gerard I know.

Vincent What do you mean?

Gerard What I said.

Vincent It couldn't have been.

Gerard It could.

Vincent It couldn't have been.

Gerard It was though.

Vincent It was when I was living in digs down Grange. It couldn't have been. He could have only been about nine. It couldn't have been. He was like a little girl. No, he was pretending to be a girl. He didn't look like a girl at all. It couldn't have been.

Gerard It was. It was when we were living over the other house.

Vincent It couldn't have been. I was in digs.

Gerard You weren't in digs.

Vincent He was only a kid. He was only . . . He couldn't have been more than about nine. He must only have been about nine.

Gerard That's right.

Vincent Don't talk soft. He was younger than you. He was about nine. It couldn't have been.

Gerard It was. I remember you looking through the window.

Vincent I was cold. You finished me.

Gerard Where are you going?

Mrs Driscoll is singing quietly.

Mrs Harte I'm going to the shop.

Vincent Mam.

Gerard Why are you going up here to the shops?

Vincent MAM!

Mrs Harte Why shouldn't I? Why are you following me?

Gerard Because I am.

Mrs Harte There's no need to follow me. Walk with me if you like. Take my arm if you want to. What is it?

Gerard It's . . .

Vincent Mam.

Mrs Harte Oh, I'm going on.

Gerard Now stop, stop walking. Stop.

Mrs Harte What?

Gerard Now let's get it clear. Straight. Now.

Vincent Mam.

Mrs Harte Hello, Mr Farrant.

Gerard What are you waving to him for?

Mrs Harte Go home. Hello, Mr Farrant. How are you?

Gerard Eh?

Vincent Mam.

Mrs Harte Go on. Go away. Gerard. Now go on. Stop it. What are you doing? Stop it, Gerard.

Vincent Mammy!

Mrs Driscoll stops singing.

Gerard Stop now. Now. Now. Let's stop it. Let's get it straight. Now. Now.

Mrs Harte I'm bad, Gerard.

Gerard I don't care. You mustn't. You're not.

Mrs Harte I'll have to sit down.

Gerard What are you doing? Tell me. What is it? What is it? What is it?

Mrs Driscoll It's all right. I'll be out in a minute.

Gerard This is unfinished. This can't finish.

Vincent Mammy.

During the last lines Mrs Harte and Mrs Driscoll are knocked to the floor.

Vincent You did, you know.

Gerard How? How?

Vincent Over the Easter holidays. It was raining, you let me in on things. You told me things. I saw things.

Gerard I finished you? And that's all you can remember, is it? A wet Easter. On the wet sand. And flecks of coal. And drizzle. Huddling underneath that old pier. You're one of those people who can't remember anything, except what suits them when the time comes, who leave the hard slog of memorising to people they find a bit quaint. To people who've found out there isn't a moment you can pin it on. Unless of course you're a rationalist and believe in original sin. Is that what you really think, then? Nothing before and nothing after. Huddling together under the old pier talking and talking.

Vincent No, but . . .

Gerard You said you loved me. You did. I made you. I realised that you did love me. Too late.

Vincent It's always too late. That's the point.

Gerard You said you loved me, then after we went to the pictures. And then lying in bed, staying in your house for a change, the kids asleep in the other corner, and the light outside, whispering and talking and talking. You kissed me to try and show you did love me and I turned away afterwards because . . . That's what I want to know, that's what interests me. You kissed me to try and show you did love me, I turned away afterwards because . . . Why? Why? What is it? What is it?

Vincent Don't ask me. Always come on. Come for a drink. I'm dry.

Gerard No.

Vincent Well, piss off, then. You're as spoiled as ever you were. Where you going?

Gerard Nowhere! You belong to me, you know.

Vincent How do you make that out?

Gerard Because I say so. That's why. You belong to me. I'm just expressing the ordinary greed. People try to eat you. They should let you eat them. So that they're not ghosts with faces you could forget. They're living inside you. Thinning you out.

Vincent Kid, we was only little.

Gerard What's age got to do with it! You knew. You were the only person that could have saved me.

Vincent Get out. From what?

Gerard From THIS!

Vincent How?

Gerard I don't know. I gave you everything I had. My selfishness. I gave you myself. But you couldn't make anything of it.

Vincent Oh, but I did. Don't you have no hope?

Gerard Do you?

Vincent I don't think in them terms.

Gerard I do. I do. I have hope.

Vincent Me. I'll just go on living till I wear away.

Gerard But who am I keeping alive in my actions? Why doesn't somebody put me down? Kill her by killing me.

Won't somebody stop it? Stop me. Kill. Kill me, will you? You won't kill her till you've killed me. Why did you get married?

Vincent What?

Gerard How fucking dare you. Why didn't you tell me?

Vincent How could I tell you?

Gerard Why didn't you find me and tell me?

Vincent How could I tell you? How could I? What? Oh, I should have asked you, should I? Should I have asked you?

Gerard Yes. Look, *you*. I never asked for it. I never asked for you. Never asked to play with you, go to school with you. Being who I am with you being who you are.

Vincent Nor me.

Gerard It was different for you.

Vincent Oh yes, it would have to be. You're so different. It would have to be.

Gerard Listen, *you*, I'm not paying out any more. I *am not*. I'm not taking any more. Who cares if you did it. I've paid out for thinking about all that. Living all that. Who cares if you did it. Did you love her? Did you hold hands? Did you walk in the park and kiss and cuddle and fool about? Hold hands, hold one hand and smoke with the other. Did you? Did you?

Vincent Yes and she was . . . She was –

Gerard Go on, you're right she was. I'm fucking glad. You had a baby. Why didn't you tell me?

Vincent You don't care about that. I know you. Do you?

And he's not even mine really. Kids aren't. Not with women.

Gerard But did you? Did you? Did you stay awake at night thinking? Did you get up and pull on your trousers and walk the streets and look up at her yellow window? Did you follow her home and look up at her window? Were you sorry and never asked for forgiveness? Did you love me? Wait for me? Want me? Did you want to run away to the haven of your mates? Did you? Did you?

Vincent Come on, son, come for a drink.

Gerard (*violently*) Get off.

Vincent You OK? What is it?

Gerard If you've got out of the habit of living in the present. Not the hysterical flash of the present, the actual present, but the present, the present that surrounds us, the present moment. The tangible immanent present they call maturity. If the present's only reality is made up of fictions of other people's lives and if the past is a location that's unsafe . . . if the past's out of perspective. If the past's . . . If you've got out of – See . . . If the past's . . . In the past sometimes you can locate pain and feel safe in its hurt – it having gone. If it's bearable you're all right, but if it's not and the past was not, the attempt to make a bearable present is made hopeless by keeping faith with the moral horrors of the past.

Vincent For Jesus' sake. What's that? That. Eh, what's that supposed to be?

Gerard Oh, how would you know? You're so stupid! You're covered in psychic fat. Psychic rind. Wrongs. Wrongs. Actual wrongs. Unnecessary sufferings that incapacitate any ability in you to change. For change. For all change. And if these were caused by other people's, dead people's, inability to deal with their present, then the route is circular and if you're like me the future is as fantasied as the past.

Vincent Piss off, Gerard, will you?

Gerard Look, *you* asked me. It's not only pictures of the past that invented me, but the literal past. The images I made of it may make me immature, but there was a literal past. Things happened that couldn't be changed. And you could have saved me. Now it's anything to get out of the present. The hideous flash of the present moment. The white sound. Chatting myself to death. Do you know, where I am they think it's going to come from you.

Vincent What?

Gerard It, I suppose.

Vincent What?

Gerard It.

Vincent Well I hope it keeps fine for them.

Gerard They *do*.

Vincent Well they've come to the wrong shop. Who are they?

Gerard Oh, people I know.

Vincent Your circle, like?

Gerard That's it.

Vincent Well tell them, look it's very late, tell them. The shop's closed. What they don't realise is that I'm a scab. Scar tissue. No blood in it. Do they, whoever they are, think . . . They don't think I'm going to *do* anything, do they? They don't think I'm going to fall for the three

card trick, do they? Do they think, any of them, that I'm
going to take any part? Your old man once said to me,
keep these open and that shut, son. We were doing a job
together. He was OK. A gentleman.

Gerard I wish he'd said something to me. Your old man
didn't say much either.

Vincent I don't think he'd got anything to say.

Gerard All he did in my remembrance is clout us once
for lighting a fire down in the shelter. But once, when
I was crying out in the street, he did stop. He never said
anything or dry my eyes or anything. But he walked up
the street with me, his hand on my shoulder, apparently
not taking any notice. But I could feel him – I could feel
he existed and it was very, very comforting. And when
I think now, that's a lot. Humanness. You know where
your old man was brought up? That's knocked down.

Vincent That's been knocked down, years.

Gerard Not one street. Not one house where people
spent their whole lives.

Vincent Don't be soft. People don't think like that.

Gerard When I was home once. Queen Street Station
had saplings growing through the broken windows.
Flowering. Couldn't they have left it?

Vincent You've got a war memorial mentality.

Gerard No I don't think so. I just know you could die
of ugliness, and that every piece of ugliness you see is
connected with more than my aesthetic displeasure. I
know it. It's connected with an immense cruelty. Cruelty
of every kind. Cruel ideas, cruel policies. It's not me. It's
impossible to put up monuments to the dead, there are too
many of them, so they're cementing up people's souls.

Vincent You ought to be a Catholic.

Gerard I would be if I wasn't one. What's going to happen though, aye? The only decent people I know are actually mad or there's a few like me wandering around abusing freedom. The other people I know are making a few bob out of being disaffected to pay off the mortgage. Or there's a few girls and sweet boys from good homes. They're nice enough.

Vincent I'd watch them. I wouldn't feel too sorry for them if I was you.

Gerard But the shop steward mentality is not enough. It's not enough.

Vincent You don't have to tell me, boy. I was a shop steward. You don't have to tell me, boy, I'm sophisticated for down here, you know. I'm separated from my wife I am. I even had a mortgage. I read *The Wizard* and J. B. Priestley. I've worked on and off since I was fourteen. I've got a trade I don't use. I've been to sea. I spent one winter scraping the dock bottom. I've worked on tugs in all weathers. I've navvied with Irish fellas I've had to beg to stop and for Christ's sake lean on their shovels so's I could have a rest. I wouldn't vote if they paid me all the stoppages they've ever took back in one lump sum. I've got some moral standards.

Gerard Well, something got to be done.

Vincent You ought to become a Catholic.

Gerard Shut up.

Vincent You can only have a sense of humour on your own terms, can't you?

Gerard How else can you have a sense of humour?

Vincent If everyone. You and me that is. If we were all to come out of our holes and put our shoulders to the wheel and say, now look, stop this, this isn't nice calling people old-age pensioners and the like. And put our shoulders to the wheel. You see I don't trust our judgement. You could be putting your shoulder to the wrong wheel.

Gerard But don't we have to do something?

Vincent There you go, you see, you won't live, will you? What you and I are prevents it. You just said. Something'll happen though.

Gerard It won't, will it?

Vincent When I was at sea.

Gerard You do remember.

Vincent You reminded me. It must have been one of my last trips, I'd got my ticket, I know that. I just had this feeling of being on deck, of coming up on deck and we were ploughing the South Seas and the clouds cleared the moon, and I thought you and me. You said to me once. Look at the moon. You were a soft bloody kid honest to my God. Why's it racing across the sky so fast? You got a bit scared, I think. It's not the moon it's the clouds being blown across it. You didn't like that either, you wanted it stuck up there not sliding about like a button. You told me how your old man used to carry you on his shoulders and run, racing the moon home to see who'd get there first. My father never did that. And you said, see the moon, and I said yes and you said as long as the moon was there then we were there. And I had to agree of course. You went on and on like a little caged thing. Till I had to agree, not agreeing with one word of your soft bloody attempts to make things permanent but not real. We were by the hedge, by the privet, you plucking, pulling out the privet flowers, pulling everything apart as usual. And one night when I was a seaman I thought of what you said. And I wished I could smell the flowers. So I thought, the moon, while she's there, you and me both. And I wanted to come home. But there isn't any home or love, only in here. (*touching his chest*) Do you know, I don't hate him. I can't blame her. But couldn't she . . . have left me out of it? Couldn't they have left me alone?

Gerard I suppose no one left them alone.

Vincent Look, they're tipping over the foreshore. You been ill? I heard you'd been ill?

Gerard There are more ways of doing it than pills and drink or banister and rope or downing caustic. Some people do it very slowly over the years.

Vincent You could say everybody if you want to look at it like that, son. How old were you when we left? Thirteen, fourteen?

Gerard Sixteen. You were seventeen. We moved straight after.

Vincent I've hardly seen you. Have I? Twice.

Gerard Three times. And once when I saw you and you didn't notice me. I crossed the road. You looked awful. And I was glad you didn't know you loved me because I couldn't love you. You're falling apart.

Vincent And what about you?

Gerard You didn't love me like I loved you. But you *did* love me. You tried to show me in your way. It was really loving of you.

Vincent No.

Gerard It was. But I was too stupid to realise, too unspeculative in the way of our class. I didn't realise that if someone *loves* you they could love you. You see, having shown you *loved* me, you could have loved me. Couldn't you? Couldn't you? You could, I know. The thing is you've never liked anyone as much as me, have you?

Vincent (*laughing*) No.

Gerard And I've never loved anyone as much as you.

Vincent It's not like that from where I see it. I haven't got your certainty. But then it's me you're talking about so I wouldn't be so sure. I can see all I may have lost in you, son. I realise you're the only person I've ever had any fun with. That you made me understand how deeply mad it all is. But do you think I'm daft? Yes, it's all possible. I went to sea for seven years. Anything's fucking possible. I was the cause of my mother pouring acid down her throat. Anything's possible. You've had no chance. I can see that. But you've had something. You can't lie to me. I can feel it. It makes me feel alive. Perhaps you can't live, but you can create life. Listen to me. What you don't or won't or can't understand is, it doesn't matter. Love. What you mean by love. What you mean by love. And you won't get your kind of love. Because you won't accept that it's true, that there's got to be some kind of give and take, some kind of basis, some kind of give and take in the ordinary way. You couldn't take this love you want if you won't accept the offer of a drink. I'm not forcing you. Even if that's what it's about. I can't. Come for a drink. I'm thirsty.

Gerard No.

Vincent Why not?

Gerard I can't. I got to go in. I've got to have my tea.

194

Vincent And me.

Gerard Or don't. Stay out.

Vincent No. I got to go in. Come for a drink.

Gerard No.

Vincent All right then. Go in.

Gerard Don't go in.

Vincent I got to.

Gerard Don't go.

Mrs Harte Gerard.

Mrs Harte and Mrs Driscoll begin to rise.

Gerard I've got to go in.

Vincent Come for a drink.

Mrs Driscoll Vincent.

Vincent I've got to go in. I'm going in. All right?

Gerard Don't.

Mrs Harte He was a lovely boy. He really was. After he drowned. His mother couldn't go up for his seaman's pay. It upset her too much. She'd rather do without it. Then if times were bad, she'd go. But not if she could help it. It wasn't pride. No, it upset her.

Gerard No French irises. No wallflowers, no new potatoes.

Vincent She used to weep bitterly, grasping the curling ends of her hair and straightening it behind her ears.

Mrs Driscoll I fancy it's inclined to rain.

Mrs Harte He was a lovely boy. Jimmy Harrington. He really was. He was ever such a comic. He used to see all the shows. Sing all the songs. Get them off to a tee. He used to cut our hair. Cut mine short for me in an Eton crop.

Vincent Swimming in the dock, light seeps through the heavy suspension of oil in the water. Head breaks through the water. Never thought one would get there. Out on to a raft. Cormorants. Or climb the cranes with Gerard. Pick up little baby pigeons.

Gerard In the other photograph, there's a deckchair, with some children piled into it. All in white. Standing behind them, leaning on the back of the deckchair is a man. He's quite vivid really. Dressed in white. Hair brushed back. White trousers and shirt with sleeves rolled back to the elbow and white sleeveless pullover and a dark tie. He's graceful, giving the impression of being tall. Like a cricketer, with graceful arms and hands and legs. None of the children is me. Where is she? I suppose, I suppose she must be taking the snap. I can't believe it.

Vincent Coming for a drink?

Gerard I can't.

Vincent Come on.

Gerard I can't. She died. She's dead.

Mrs Harte What, love?

Gerard She's dead, she died.

Mrs Harte Do you want a cup of coffee?

Vincent Come on.

Gerard She is.

Mrs Harte I'll make it with all milk.

Vincent Gerard!

Gerard What?

Vincent You coming out?

Gerard Vincent! You going out, Vincent?

Vincent You coming out, Gerard?

Loudly, together:

Gerard	Vincent!
Mrs Harte	Gerard!
Mrs Driscoll	Vincent!
Vincent	Gerard!

Gerard Try but can't. Won't but can. Will but can't. Shall but don't.

KICK FOR TOUCH

For Andrew

Kick for Touch was first produced, in repertory with *Small Change*, on the Cottesloe stage of the National Theatre, London, on 15 February 1983, with the following cast:

Joe Kenneth Cranham
Jim James Hazeldine
Eileen Jane Lapotaire

Directed by Peter Gill

Characters

Joe

Jim

Eileen

One

A table and four chairs, centre. A door centre at the back. Joe, Jim and Eileen. Eileen sitting at the table facing the door.

Joe You been in long?

Jim No.

Joe You just beat me to it. I only been out for a packet of fags. Did you get in alright?

Jim I come round the back.

Joe Aye. I left it for you. I thought you might come when I was out. You eaten?

Jim No. I only just come in.

Joe I thought you might have eaten on the train.

Jim No. You?

Joe Aye. I didn't know whether to expect you or not.

Jim Why d'you leave the back door, then?

Joe In case you come.

Jim Oh.

  Pause.

Where is he?

Joe Out playing, I should think. He'll be in in a minute.

Jim Don't you know where he is?

Joe What do you mean? Of course I know where he is.

Jim How's he doing?

Joe Oh he's fine. He's champion. You wait till you see him. He shouldn't be long.

Pause.

Jim I tried phoning you in work. I phoned next door but they must have been out.

Joe What d'you want to do that for?

Jim They didn't seem to mind.

Joe What d'you want to phone me there for? I'm nowhere near the phone. The phone's in the office.

Jim Well, they knew who you were. The bloke went to find you.

Joe Don't phone us in work.

Jim Why not?

Joe Look, don't phone us in work, alright?

Jim Alright. Alright.

Pause.

You don't alter much, do you?

Joe What?

Jim I said you don't alter a lot.

Joe What's there to alter me?

Pause.

Shall I get you something to eat?

Jim No. I won't bother, thanks.

Joe You'd better have something. What do you want?

Jim I'll get it.

Joe I'll get it. What do you want?

Jim I don't want anything.

Joe Right-o.

Pause.

I'll put the kettle on in a minute.

Jim Right-o.

Pause.

Did you play on Saturday?

Joe Aye, I had a game.

Jim Wonder they let you play, an old man like you.

Joe Oh aye.

Jim What team?

Joe What you mean what team? The first team. What team!

Jim The first team. They must be hard up then. If they picked you for the first team. Who'd you play for? Eh? The Reserves? That's more like it. How are the mighty fallen.

Joe It's a game.

Jim Aye.

Pause.

Joe I had a game of rugby the week before last.

Jim Get out.

Joe I did. I enjoyed it. I played in the pack.

Jim Blimey.

Joe Have you been playing?

Jim No, I haven't.

Joe Why not?

Jim Nowhere to play. No one to play for.

Joe Oh.

Pause.

I was up your way.

Jim When?

Joe Ooo . . . fortnight ago it must be.

Jim Why didn't you call in?

Joe I should have.

Jim Why didn't you?

Joe I will next time.

Jim Oh yeah.

Joe I will. I'll come up soon.

Jim You could get a bus up.

Joe Yes. I suppose I could.

Jim And it's much cheaper and quicker. With the motorway and the bridge.

Pause.

Couldn't you?

Joe Aye.

Jim You won't.

Joe I will. There's talk of getting a trip up.

Pause.

Jim You going out?

Joe Well, I was going out.

Jim Well, don't let me stop you.

Joe No, I won't.

Eileen Don't go out.

Jim Where you going?

Joe For a drink. I don't know.

Eileen Don't go out.

Jim Have you signed on?

Joe What?

Jim Don't get shirty. I'm only asking. Have you?

Joe Of course I have.

Jim Have you?

Joe Of course I have.

Jim I hate signing on.

Joe Well, you're lucky then, aren't you?

Jim How d'you make that out?

Joe You don't have to sign on.

Jim No, but I have signed on.

Joe When was the last time you signed on?

Jim I don't know. Anyway, you needn't be signing on.

Joe Look don't go on, eh? Alright? I'll sign on tomorrow.

Jim I knew you hadn't signed on. That's just like you that is. Why haven't you signed on?

Joe I have, I'm kidding you. I signed on today.

Eileen Don't go out.

Joe Two hours I was in there. What a place.

Jim Still, at least they send you your money.

Joe Of course they send you your money. You still have to sign on though.

Jim Only once a week.

Joe Things have vastly improved. Anyway, I've got the chance of working a fiddle.

Jim How's that?

Joe Fella I know's got a job contracting.

Jim You wanna watch they don't catch you.

Joe How they gonna catch me?

Jim You wanna be careful all the same.

  Pause.

Joe It was packed in there today. Everyone smoking and bloody coughing. I hate signing on. I hate it.

Jim Go on, it's not as bad as all that.

Joe How would you know?

Jim Well, it's got to be better than it used to be.

Joe Has it?

Jim Well, what you chuck the job for then?

Joe Because I wanted to, right?

  Pause.

Bloke behind me in the queue said, what I hates is post offices.

Jim I hate post offices.

Joe The fella in front of me was chuckling. What's up, I said. I'll have to try my old job if it comes down to it, he said. God knows what his old job was. He looked wrecked from drink. Can't see him getting a job. God knows what he used to do that made him like that. Another bloke said, one pound fifty it cost me in fares to get there and back and they'll let me know. Let me know, mind you. One fella was letting them have it. Poor kid behind the counter didn't know what hit him. Do you think I've got no better place to go, he shouted. No better things to do than to come here on time. Young fella come in. You should have seen him. I've seen some sights in my time but you should've seen him. Filthy clothes and big sore eyes in a dirty head. He shambled round and then out again. Then another bloke come in. He'd been on a right razzle. Skittled out of his head. Come on down the queue, some fellas shouted, but he stood where he was, leant against the radiator and he said, you only die one time he said. You don't die twice. You only die one time. You don't see daylight no more. We've all got to go, haven't we, he said. I've got six months to live. I signed on, had a pint, came home and went to bed.

Eileen Will you?

Joe Look, just keep that quiet a bit, will you? Let's have a bit less of that, shall we? How about shutting your trap for a change? How about just keeping quiet?

Eileen Don't go out.

Joe I'm going out.

Eileen You bloody bloody sod.

Joe I'm going out, right.

Eileen You bloody bloody . . . You swine. You know that's what you are, don't you?

Joe Look, just keep *that* quiet a bit, will you? Let's have a bit less of that shall we? How about shutting your trap for a change? How about just keeping quiet? Look, let's get this straight. I'm going out.

Pause.

Jim He's out late, isn't he? It must be getting dark, you know.

Joe Aye, I'll have to go and get him, I suppose.

Jim I'll go.

Joe No, I'll go. He'll be back in a minute, anyway.

Jim Has he had tea?

Joe Of course he's had his tea. He had it ages ago.

Jim Who's going to mind him?

Joe The girl next door will come in. She's working for her exams. She's glad of the peace and quiet.

Jim I'll mind him.

Joe Aren't you coming out?

Jim Nah, I'm too tired.

Jim Where are you going, anyway?

Joe Nowhere. For a pint. Nowhere. Ah, I don't think I'll bother.

Jim Go on. Don't let me stop you.

Joe No, I don't think I will.

Jim I'll look after him.

Joe No, the girl next door's coming in. Anyway, you'd keep him up.

Jim I wouldn't.

Joe She's reading all what you used to read. I think she's glad of the peace and quiet.

Jim Go on.

Joe No, I won't bother.

Eileen Please, Jimmy.

Jim Don't let me stop you.

Joe No, honest.

Jim Joe.

Eileen Jim.

Joe No, honest.

Eileen Please.

Jim Where you drinking?

Joe Oh, nowhere.

Jim Don't you drink down the end?

Joe Not much.

Eileen Jim.

Jim I'll see to him.

Eileen Please. Jim. Jimmy. Let me come back with you. Please.

Jim I can't, love. How can I?

Eileen Please, Jim.

Jim I can't. Don't be stupid. I can't.

Eileen You won't.

Jim I can't.

    Pause.

What is it? What's the matter? Tell me. Eh? Don't. Don't, love.

Eileen Don't look at me, please.

Jim Tell me. What is it?

Eileen Don't look at me. Please. Please, Jim, let me come back with you. Please.

Jim I can't. You know I can't.

Pause.

Joe I think I'd better go and get him.

Jim I think you better had an' all.

Joe What do you mean?

Jim Nothing.

Pause.

Has he had his tea?

Joe I told you he had his tea.

Jim Alright.

Joe He's had his tea. He's had his tea. Alright?

Jim Alright. Alright. What's all this about? I only asked.

Joe And I told you.

Pause.

Where's your gear?

Jim In the passage.

Joe Do you want it taking up?

Jim No, it's alright. I'll take it up later.

Pause.

Why didn't you call in?

Joe I told you I meant to.

Jim Yeah.

Jim I did.

Jim Oh aye.

Joe Well you haven't made a habit of visiting, have you?

Jim I'm busy.

Joe So am I busy.

Jim Well that makes two ignorant bastards then, doesn't it?

Joe It does.

Pause.

Jim When you going to finish the painting?

Joe In the kitchen?

Jim Yes.

Joe Yeah, I'll have to.

Pause.

Jim I don't know why you don't go in for this house.

Joe No, I know.

Jim You should, you know.

Joe I should, I know.

Jim You should.

Joe I know I should.

Pause.

Jim She told me you didn't understand her. That you never really understood her.

Joe She really didn't understand me.

Jim I don't understand you.

Joe What's there to understand? I'm straightforward enough.

Jim She told me she didn't understand you either.

Joe Oh, did she? Well, we were made for each other then, weren't we?

Pause.

She used to say, Oh I wish Jimmy was here, she'd say. Often she'd say that. And if you was here when I come in home from work I'd say, Hello kid, what time you get in? Been in long? Hiya kid. Hiya son. Here he is, she'd say. Make a fuss. We'd make a fuss, wouldn't we? I'd say.

Pause.

Anyway, what's the point of going in for this house? They're clearing all this eventually.

Jim They're not, are they?

Joe That's what I heard.

Jim They won't knock this down yet.

Joe Anyway, they can't put you out anyway, can they? Not without finding you somewhere else first? Can they?

Jim I don't know. I shouldn't think so.

Joe That's what I heard. That's what he reckons next door the other way. Big-mouth.

Jim Oh aye. How is he?

Joe Still knows it all. You know that they'd all been laid off?

Jim Get out.

Joe Didn't you know?

Jim I must have done, I suppose. All of them?

Joe Do you know how much he got?

Jim Must have been a tidy packet – he's worked there long enough.

Joe Five thousand pounds.

Jim Not bad.

Joe Not bad! Mind you he's very anti-union, he says, very anti-union, he told me.

Jim What did you say?

Pause.

Mind you, how long is that going to last?

Joe What, you mean he's getting a second car, he said.

Jim How old is he – fifty?

Joe He must be over fifty.

Jim Is he working?

Joe Don't worry, he'll get work.

Jim Oh, will he?

Joe What you talking about? I wouldn't mind five thousand pounds.

Jim Well, you should have stayed over the works then.

Pause.

Joe What's the time? I'll have to go and get him. He's getting too much of it. He'll know it if I have to go and get him.

Jim Oh.

Joe What do you mean, oh? He knows he's supposed to be in. He can be a little bugger. No, he's a good kid. Funny, everyone says that. You can't hold out against him. But he's getting too much of it. Last weekend I had to go looking for him. I went all over the fields. He wanders for miles. Met him on my way back, sauntering down the lane, grass in his mouth. Miles away. Said he couldn't see what I was on about.

Jim You can talk. You was always on the run.

Joe Aye.

Jim They blamed me when you went to London on the train. Copper had to travel back with you.

Pause.

Joe You could have come with me.

Jim How could I have come with you? How old was I?

Joe You'd have been alright with me.

Jim Oh yeah. I was going to believe that.

Pause.

Tell us about him.

Joe What do you mean, tell us about him?

Jim How is he?

Joe He's fine. He's champion.

Jim Go on, Joe.

Joe Don't be such a big kid.

Jim Tell us. Tell us.

Joe What's there to tell? He's fine. He still holds my hand on our way – him to school – me to work. Likes chatting. Sometimes I see him look puzzled. His eyes are deep set. Needs plenty . . . to get plenty of sleep. Likes a joke. I got him a fretsaw. Does what he likes really with him. Want to ask forgiveness if he cries. Oh, don't cry. Try to tell him things. You know. He's clever. Well, not. Yes, he's good in his class. Likes soccer. Manchester. Rubbish. Fulham. Rubbish. When he was asleep at first used to wake him. Hold a mirror to his mouth. He's a heavy breather, sleeps with his mouth open. I have to stop myself sometimes holding on to him. I think that's why he goes off. Try not to interfere with his independence. But I want to hold on to him see. If ever he runs to me, which he still does – perhaps even more, up in the air. Once I thought I saw him down the other street, where the houses are being pulled down. There was a door open into the house. I thought I saw his mother, her sleeves rolled up, drying another boy by the fire. Another boy, stronger-limbed than him. Funny. I've got to take him to the dentist.

Eileen Are you ready, Joe? Where's my bag? Joe.

Joe What?

Eileen Come on, if you're coming.

Joe No, I don't think I will.

Eileen Come on. You're ready now. Come on. You'll like it when we get there.

Joe OK. Where's my fags?

Eileen I don't know. There they are.

Joe Have you got any cigarettes?

Eileen I'll buy some. Come on.

Joe These are mine, right?

Eileen Alright. Alright. Honest. Come on.

Joe Are my shoes clean?

Eileen Yes. Now come on. What's the matter?

Pause.

Joe You'll be there won't you?

Eileen Of course I will.

Joe If I come with you, you'll stay with me, won't you? No leaving me, and going off talking to everyone else, will you?

Eileen Don't be silly. Of course I won't. Do I look alright?

Joe Fine.

Eileen Oh.

Joe You look fine. But I'd rather your blue dress.

Eileen Shall I change?

Joe No. You look fine. I just like you in the blue dress.

Eileen I can change.

Joe No. You look fine, honest. Great. You ready? I just like you in the blue dress.

Eileen I don't know what he thinks of me. What does he think about me? Do you know? Does he like me, do you think?

Jim Of course he's bound to like you, isn't he?

Eileen Is he? I don't know.

Jim Of course he is bound to, isn't he?

Eileen Well, why doesn't he say anything then? Has he said anything, Jimmy?

Jim No.

Eileen Why not?

Jim Ask him, don't ask me.

Joe What did she say?

Jim What do you mean, what did she say? She said plenty.

Joe Did she say anything about me?

Jim Nothing at all.

Joe Nothing at all?

Jim Nothing at all.

Joe She must have said something.

Jim She didn't.

Joe She must have done.

Jim Well, why don't you ask her?

Joe I did ask her. But I wanted to know what she said to you.

Jim Why?

Joe Because I want to hear it from you. From you. From you. Right? What she said from you.

Eileen Are you going?

Jim I'll have to.

Eileen So long then.

Jim When will I see you?

Eileen When you come round.

Jim Don't be like that. When can I see you?

Eileen Well, you're both playing on Saturday aren't you?

Jim Can't I see you before then?

Eileen No.

Pause.

I don't know . . . How?

Jim Phone me.

Eileen How can I phone you?

Jim You going back to work?

Eileen Of course I am.

Jim Phone me from work.

Eileen Where? What time?

Jim When I've finished. About six o'clock. Ring the phone box. I'll wait outside.

Eileen I don't know the number.

Jim You can find the number.

Eileen How?

Jim Look it up. Ring the phone box, OK?

Eileen I might.

Jim I'll be waiting outside.

Joe He got that job, then.

Eileen Did he? He didn't tell me. Is he going?

Joe I suppose he is.

Eileen Oh. Well.

Joe Why's he going? Did he say anything?

Eileen Feels he must, I suppose.

Joe He mightn't go.

Eileen I hope he don't go. But he might feel he has to go.

Joe Don't you care?

Eileen Yes. But it's his affair, isn't it?

Jim Come on.

Eileen Don't, Jim.

Jim Why not?

Eileen You mustn't.

Jim Why not?

Eileen Don't be silly. Jimmy. Don't. Joe will be in.

Jim Well, will you come out then? Will you?

Eileen I can't.

Jim Will you? Please. Will you?

Eileen Shh. Yes. I'll come. Now stop.

Jim Tonight?

Eileen I don't know. Alright.

Jim Honest?

Eileen Yes. I said.

Jim I'll meet you about eight o'clock.

Eileen Where?

Jim In town.

Eileen Alright, where?

Jim By the station.

Eileen Alright. Don't keep me waiting.

Jim How are you going to find a way?

Eileen I'll find a way, don't you worry.

Joe Have Jim gone?

Eileen You've just missed him.

Joe I didn't see him. Oh, I wanted to see him.

Eileen Well, you'll see him tomorrow, won't you?

Joe Aye. What's for tea? Where is he?

Eileen Look, what's that? Come here. How did you do that?

Jim You've seen it.

Eileen I haven't. It goes right through your hair.

Jim Yeah.

Eileen How did you do that?

Jim I don't know. I was smaller than him when it happened.

Eileen *He*'s all cuts. How did you do it?

Jim I don't know.

Eileen You must know.

Jim I don't. Joe would remember more than me. I had to have stitches. I remember that. It was before we got separated.

Eileen You must remember it.

Jim I don't. I don't remember it. Not really. Joe would remember better than me. Why don't you ask him?

Eileen He don't tell me anything. You know that.

Jim I don't. Ask Joe. I can't tell you anything. I can't remember anything.

Joe All the same, she shouldn't have done that.

Jim She told me that you didn't understand her. That you've never really understood her.

Joe I was lucky, mind. There's not many people that was lucky like I was. When I come out first I was no different to all the other animals. It was her doing. Still I don't think she should have done that.

Eileen You shouldn't have lent me that record, that book. We shouldn't have watched that play, that film.

Jim I thought you were going to make some tea?

Joe Aye, I'll put the kettle on.

Eileen When I'm with you people think I must be so happy. So happy.

Joe Are you sleeping with him or me?

Jim I don't mind.

Joe You'd better sleep with me, I think.

Jim OK.

Eileen They do. They do.

Joe I'm in the back bedroom, mind.

Eileen Everything I was brought up to believe in has gone. There's no heaven and no God. And if there was I'm sure I'm not fit to meet him.

Joe Hark.

Jim What?

Joe There's the side door. Yeah, there he is. Is that you? Eh. Where you been? Don't stay out there, Jimmy's here.

Jim Bring my bag. I've got something for you. Alright?

Joe And put the kettle on, Jim. OK?

Two

Joe, Jim and Eileen sitting at the table. There is a school blazer on the back of the downstage chair. A pair of boy's shoes on the table, socks on the floor. Tea cups. Joe is holding a boy's shirt, vest and pants.

Jim I thought he was a farm labourer.

Joe Don't be silly. He worked in the steel works.

Jim Funny, I always thought you lived on a farm.

Joe She came from a farm and he used to be a farm labourer and there was a farm up the lane but we didn't live on a farm.

Jim Then how come I thought that you lived on a farm?

Joe That's because when you visited us he used to walk us up the lane to see the farm where he used to work.

Jim Aye, I can remember the farm. I can remember them. And the house. He was a nice man.

Joe He was. And she was nice.

Jim He had a garden.

Joe He did. He liked his garden. And so did she. I can see her now by the clothes prop with the pegs in her pocket, the clothes wrung out in a bucket by her feet. Or him at the end. Smoking. I always seem to be by one or the other of them. Sometimes they're together, sometimes single, or sometimes I'm under the currant bushes between his end of the garden and hers. Or sometimes she's down his end and they're pulling the line up into the wind. He always used to smoke his pipe outside. Out the back or in the shed. Never indoors. I used to pretend that I'd been with them much longer. Not that I'd been born there, mind you. But that instead of being brought up on the bus and then handed over, that he'd brought me home with him one night unexpectedly when I was very little – carried me inside his overcoat.

Jim Oh aye.

Joe Once we'd all been caned because no one'd own to having pinched something. When I come home from school dinner time I told her and, though she was a bit hesitant at first, she was all for going down the school. The old man said he'd come, but first he asked if I know who'd done it. Well, I did know. Why didn't you tell then, he said. I was shocked. Well then, he said, you made your choice and the teacher made his and he caned you. And he put his cap on and went back to work. They were a nice old couple. Very good to me they were.

Jim Pity you lost touch with them, really.

Joe Yeah. I used to keep in touch.

Jim Why don't you get in touch with them again?

Joe Nah. They were old enough then.

Jim I would.

Pause.

He must be asleep.

Joe We'd soon know if he wasn't.

Jim He's good, isn't he?

Joe He is. These'll have to be washed. There's nothing here he can wear again. He's a tyke. Where's your gear?

Jim Upstairs.

Joe Do you want anything washed?

Jim No. I haven't got much with me.

Pause.

Why isn't he playing rugby?

Joe Well, he will if he wants to. He's young yet.

Jim I was playing rugby at his age.

Joe Didn't turn you into much of a player.

Jim Oh aye. I could convert any ball you touched down.

Pause.

When I went up, he asked if he could come back with me.

Joe Oh aye.

Jim I had to promise to ask you.

Joe He won't go, Jim. Not that he's ever in. But he won't go.

Pause.

Aren't you going to eat anything?

Jim I'll have another cup of tea.

Joe You want more than a cup of tea.

Jim No. That'll do me fine.

Pause.

Above the house there was a track, wasn't there?

Joe Yeah, and above that was slate and above that was the top. I used to get up there and you used to look back at the house and the farm. (*He finds a sheet of paper. Laughs.*)

Jim What's that?

Joe This.

Jim What is it?

Joe Alright, listen.

Jim. James. Jimmy.
Club: Liverpool.
Ground: Anfield Road, Liverpool.
Manager: Bob Paisley.
Captain: Emlyn Hughes.
The team of Liverpool:
1. Ray Clemence (England)
2. Tommy Smith (England)
3. Joey Jones (Wales)
4. Phil Thompson (England)
5. Ray Kennedy (England)
6. Emlyn Hughes (England)
7. Kenny Dalglish (Scotland)
8. Jimmy Case (England)
9. Steve Heighway (Eire)
10. David Fairclough (England under-23)
11. Ian Callaghan (England)

They both laugh.

Eileen What's wrong with you two?

Joe What?

Eileen You been drinking?

Joe What?

Eileen Have you?

Joe Me?

Eileen You.

Joe Not me. You know me.

Eileen How many pints did you have?

Joe How many we have?

Jim Oo, not many.

Joe Two. We had two.

Jim Aye. Two we had.

Eileen Two!

Joe Honest, we would have left earlier but Jim met a friend.

Jim Did I?

Joe Fella come in, wouldn't let us go. We been in ages. Jim fell asleep. Fell akip.

Eileen You surprise me.

Jim Yeah. (*Goes to sleep.*)

Eileen Don't go to sleep, Jimmy. You're not staying here.

Joe Yes he can.

Eileen No he can't.

Joe He can go in with him.

Jim No. I'll sleep down here.

Eileen You're not, you've got your own bed. Come on you've got to be up.

Joe Now . . . now . . . now.

Jim is asleep.

Is he asleep?

Eileen He is. I'm going up. Look at him.

Joe Don't laugh at him.

Eileen I'm not laughing at him. Big kid.

Joe Don't say that about him.

Eileen I've said nothing about him. I wish you were more like him, I tell you that.

Joe Have he got that job?

Eileen I don't know.

Joe He hasn't said anything.

Eileen Hasn't he?

Joe Will he take it?

Eileen I don't know. Look at this scar in his hair. When did he get it?

Joe He's always had it. (*Yawns.*)

Eileen Don't go to sleep.

   Pause.

Goodnight.

Joe Goodnight.

Eileen Don't be long.

   He sleeps. She looks at them, turning to go. Jimmy wakes.

Jim Oh. Hello.

Eileen I don't know. Goodnight.

Jim Don't go. Sit down.

Eileen What?

Jim Sit down. Talk to me.

Eileen No.

Jim Sit down. Don't be like that.

She sits.

Is he asleep? Nice this. I envy you. Look at him.

Eileen He's uncomfortable. I'd better wake him.

Jim Don't. Just sit for a bit.

Pause.

Do you love him, our Joe?

Eileen Don't you?

Jim That's not what I said.

Eileen Sometimes I don't, like tonight. Nor you much.

Jim But you do really.

Eileen Of course I do.

Jim Do you honest?

Eileen Don't be silly, of course I do.

Jim That's nice for you.

Eileen What's matter with you?

Jim Nothing.

Eileen Look at him. I'd better wake him.

Jim Don't.

Eileen I'm tired. I've got to be up. And you have. Joe. Joe. (*waking him*)

Joe Oh, hello.

Eileen Come on. Up you get, and you, Jimmy. I don't know why you let him drink.

Joe He's not a kid, are you?

Jim No, am I?

Joe catches hold of her.

Eileen Now don't act so bloody daft.

Joe Come here.

Eileen Stop it, Joe. You'll wake him.

Joe He's awake. Oh, is he asleep?

Eileen Of course he's asleep.

Joe Let's get him up.

Eileen You will not.

Joe Come here.

Eileen Stop it now. Stop.

Joe Come on, come on.

They chase and catch her between them. Pause.

What happened?

Eileen Nothing happened. I told you nothing happened. Don't go on about it, please.

Joe I can believe that.

Eileen Nothing happened. Don't be silly.

Joe I can believe that. I'll have him though, I will.

Eileen Nothing happened.

Joe Then what did you tell me for?

Eileen I wish I hadn't.

Joe I wish you bloody hadn't an' all.

Eileen I was frightened, you see.

Joe Of Jimmy. Ha, ha.

Eileen Of what might happen. Of what could happen.

Joe You said nothing happened. What happened?

Eileen Nothing happened. I didn't say anything happened.

Joe Then what did you tell me for?

Eileen I wish I hadn't.

Joe I wish you bloody hadn't an' all.

Eileen I should have kept my mouth shut.

Joe You should have. You should have kept it well shut.

Jim What did he say?

Eileen Nothing much.

Jim What did you want to tell him for?

Eileen I had to.

Jim Why?

Eileen I was frightened.

Jim What of?

Eileen Of what might happen, of what could happen.

Jim What could happen?

Eileen I don't know.

Jim Then what did you tell him for?

Eileen I wish I hadn't now.

Jim What's he going to do?

Eileen Nothing. He's not going to do anything.

Jim Not that I'm worried. I don't care what he does. I'm ready for him whatever he does.

Eileen I wish I'd kept quiet about it now.

Jim I wish you had too.

Eileen I should have kept my own counsel.

Jim Aren't you going out?

Joe No, I don't think I'll bother after all.

Jim Go on.

Joe Nah.

Jim Look, don't stop because of me. Go on. Joe. Aren't you going out? Alright, stay in. Look. I don't mind. Honestly. Don't let that stop you. I know I'm not long in but don't let that stop you. Not that it would stop you. Unless you were short of a couple of bob. I don't mind, honest I don't. Do you want the lend of a couple of quid?

Joe No.

Jim Go on. You flush then? You can't be. Go on.

Joe Thanks. Why don't you come?

Jim Where you going?

Joe What does it matter where I'm going? Why don't you just come out for Jesus' sake?

Jim Well, don't fly off the handle.

Joe Well, don't be so bloody childish then.

Jim You're so . . . You're so . . .

Pause.

Eileen I've come back.

Joe I can see that. Give you your marching orders, did he?

Eileen Don't be so silly. Where is he?

Joe Who? Where is he? Oh, where is he?

Eileen Look, don't make it impossible.

Joe Alright. Alright. Sit down. You look tired.

Eileen I am tired.

Pause.

Is he alright?

Joe Of course he's alright. What did you expect him to be? We managed. Fine. Thanks.

Eileen I wrote.

Joe I know. I read it.

Eileen What did you tell him?

Joe Very much what you wrote. He's alright.

Eileen Joe. You don't know what you're like.

Joe Look, don't start.

She goes to him. He moves away. Pause.

How's Jimmy?

Eileen Fine. He was very kind.

Joe He fucking should be. Very kind. Fuck me.

Eileen He told me things I didn't know.

Joe Like what?

236

Eileen Things. I did know really. Joe, I don't know what to do. Don't be like that.

Joe I'm not being like anything. Sit down. And don't for fuck's sake cry or I'll fucking do you.

He cries. She goes to him.

No. Fuck off. Right?

Eileen Oh dear. Oh God.

Joe He'll be in soon. Let's get ourselves sorted out, shall we?

Pause.

I wouldn't like to talk to her. Just see her. She might be too shy, I know that. But I'd like to see her. Him. I wonder what's like up there now. But it would be no good. They must be old by now. They might be dead.

Jim They won't be dead.

Joe No, I suppose not.

Jim Why don't you go up there, then?

Joe Yeah.

Jim I would.

Joe I should.

Jim I would.

Eileen I can't go through with this, Joe.

Joe Aye. I heard you.

Eileen I can't, Joe. I'm serious.

Joe I know you're serious. Get rid of it then.

Eileen Don't be such a pig.

Joe Well, what do you want me to say? Have it. I don't mind. I'd be glad. I'd be glad, I've told you.

Eileen I can't.

Joe You'll have to make your mind up.

Eileen I can't.

Joe Well, I don't care anyway. I shouldn't think it's mine.

Eileen Whose else is it?

Joe If it was mine you wouldn't care. You're scared, that's what you are. Bloody scared. Think I don't know you? I know you. You're so clever, thinking you know me. I know you. You. What you're scared about.

Eileen I can't have another baby.

Joe One kid. You've got one bloody kid and you're scared of another. Don't make sense. Not a bit of sense it don't make. You're not sure, are you? That's what it is.

Eileen Stop it, Joe.

Joe Have it. Get rid of it. I've got my kid.

Eileen If it is your kid.

Joe Oh aye. Oh aye.

Eileen What you so bloody smug about? You said it. How do you know it's yours? You smug swine.

Joe Stop it.

Eileen You stop it. (*to Joe*) I wish it *was* his. (*to Jim*) I wish it *was* yours. I wish the other had been his. I do, I do. (*to Jim*) I wish the other had been yours. I do, I do.

Jim Don't.

Eileen I don't. I don't. But I wish you'd both leave me alone.

Jim Don't. Don't.

Joe I'll kill you, you fucking cow, trying to wind me up like that. I know you when you're winding me up.

Eileen Going to hit me now, are you?

Joe I wouldn't give you the fucking satisfaction. I don't care about you enough to bloody hit you. I'll get him, though. I will. I've had him before now, you know.

Eileen Well we know why that is.

Joe Why?

Eileen That's because you care more for him than you care for me.

Joe The only bugger I care about is me. Right? Me and him.

Eileen Joe. It isn't. It isn't. We . . . nothing like that.

Joe Shut up, I don't want to hear you talk about it. Shut up. I'll put you out on the street.

Eileen You'll what?

Joe Get out. Go on, get out, before I put you out. I'll put you fucking right out.

Eileen You won't put me out. Who do you think you are? What kind of stunt do you think you're pulling? I'd go first. I'd bloody go first.

Joe Oh, stop acting childish.

Pause.

Jim Are you crying?

Eileen No.

Jim What's the matter?

Eileen I caught my hand in the door.

Jim Give it here.

Pause.

Your hair's dirty.

Eileen Don't.

Jim And your eyes are red, and your skin . . . But you're beautiful, you know. I like you, you know.

Pause.

Eileen Look at my hands.

Jim Yeah.

Pause.

Eileen Thanks.

Jim What about me?

Eileen Oh, you're a beautiful boy.

Jim Am I?

Eileen You are.

Jim And am I good?

Eileen Well, you're good when you're asleep.

Jim Kiss me. Kiss me.

Eileen No.

Jim Please.

Eileen No, I've stopped crying now.

Joe I'd better soak his football gear too.

Jim Not going out then?

Joe No. I'll stop in. He's got a game Wednesday. I hope they'll dry. It's a bit late now.

Jim You can if you want to. Honest.

Joe No, there's all this to do. (*indicating the boy's clothing*)

Jim I'll do it.

Joe No. Honest.

Eileen Take me down there, Jim. Will you?

Jim Don't be silly. He's having a drink. You know he likes a drink by himself.

Eileen I'll go down there by myself. I will.

Jim Don't be silly. Stop it. He's like that. He's just gone for a drink. Leave it.

Eileen Why is he like this?

Jim He's always been like it. He threw the radio out of the window once because his team lost.

Eileen I hate this. All of it.

Jim Do you?

Eileen You're like your brother, you are.

Jim So they say.

Eileen Taking sides.

Jim I'm not taking sides. Not his side nor your side.

Eileen I can't make you out, the pair of you.

Jim Oh?

Eileen I can't.

Jim Can't you?

Eileen No. I can't.

Jim He thinks I had it better than him. I think he had it better than me. You see?

Eileen No.

Jim I can't forgive him for taking so long to like me. For taking so long to forgive me. I hate him for that. I do. I don't think he ever liked me. I don't think I like him. I think really I don't like you.

   Pause.

Do you want me to walk down and see where he is?

Eileen If you like. I don't care.

   Pause.

Jim You wonder what it is about you that made them do it. That's what it amounts to. What it is about you. What it is about you that made it happen. It was bad at one time. The feeling. Very bad. Very. I like you in that dress. You know it's not you. But all the same you feel that it must be. It never goes away really. You must. Don't let it. Mm mm mm. You. Well, you find a way. You er, er. At least I have. I don't know about Joe. Don't, love. OK.

Eileen Where does this all leave me?

Jim Don't, love. OK.

   Pause.

Joe I'm going, then.

Jim Oh aye.

Joe I can't stay in, Jim.

Jim Who's asking you to?

Joe Do you mind?

Jim Why should I mind? Go on. You know you like a drink by yourself.

Joe Do you want anything brought back?

Jim No.

Pause.

Joe You'll watch him, then?

Jim You know I will.

Joe He won't wake.

Jim I'll be alright.

Joe Do you want a sandwich before I go?

Jim Aye. OK.

Joe What d'you want?

Jim What you got?

Eileen Why don't you leave me alone? The both of you.

Three

Jim, Joe and Eileen as before. On the table the shoes and socks from the last scene. Another pair of shoes some sizes smaller is on the table near them. Eileen with a small boy's shirt, vest and pants.

Eileen We waited for you. But I thought I'd better put him up.

   Pause.

I'd better see if he's settled, I think. What kept you? Joe? Oh well . . .

Jim Do you want me to see if he's alright?

Joe If you want to. But he'll be OK. I'll go up in a minute. He generally has the clothes off by now.

   Joe sings Elvis Presley's 'Are You Lonesome Tonight' throughout what follows.

Jim (*quoting from* On the Waterfront) D'you like beer? What? I bet you never had a glass of beer. You ever had a glass of beer? You wanna have one with me? I know a nice little dump down there got a special entrance for ladies all like that, come on. I won't hurt you, come on. Yeah? Good.

   He throws the imaginary pigeon he has been holding up in the air, imitating the sound of its wings. Joe is still singing. Jim quotes Julie Harris from East of Eden.

Is she following you? Girls follow you around. Don't they, Cal? (*He impersonates James Dean's reaction.*)

I found this ring that Dad gave my new mother so I took it and threw it in the river. I thought you'd like that. (*He reverts to* On the Waterfront.) You don't have to be afraid of me, I'm not going to bite you. I guess they don't let you walk with fellas where you bin. Are you training to be a nun? Wait a second. Where is that? Where's that, up . . . where is that? (*He pretends to put on Eva Marie Saint's imaginary glove.*) The country? I don't like the country. The crickets make me nervous.

Joe begins the spoken section of the Presley song. Jim reverts to On the Waterfront.

That wasn't him, Charlie, it was you. You remember that night in the Garden, you came down my dressing room you said, kid, this ain't your night we're going for the price on Wilson, you remember that, this ain't your night. My night, I could've taken Wilson apart. So what happens he gets the title shot outdoors in the ball-park and what do I get? A one-way ticket to Palookaville. You was my brother, Charlie, you shoulda looked out for me a little bit. You shoulda taken care of me just a little bit so I wouldn't have to take them dives for the short-end money. You don't understand, I coulda had class, I coulda been a contender, I coulda been somebody instead of a bum which is what I am, let's face it. It was you, Charlie.

Joe finishes the spoken section of the song. Pause. Jim goes back to East of Eden *again.*

I've got something to show you, I think you'll find it very interesting. Maybe our mother didn't die and go to heaven after all, Aaron. Maybe she didn't, maybe she's alive some place. Remember when we were kids you used to make up stories about her, you said she must've looked like heaven's youngest angel, remember that? Remember that time I shot that rabbit and you cried and you said, you said that she woulda cried too 'cos she was so tender-hearted and you said I was bad, you remember that? I just wanna show you something, it's not going to take very long. What's the matter, you afraid? Can you look at the truth, just once, uh? Come on, you can look at the truth just once can't you, uh? Come on, come on, I wanna show you something, it won't take very long. (*He pulls Joe out of his chair.*)

Joe No. Get off. Get off, Jimmy. (*throwing him off*) GET OFF. (*Pause. Quotes from* The Man who Shot Liberty Vallance.) Looks like we got ourselves a ladies' man.

> *They sit. Joe starts to sing the Everly Brothers' song 'Dream'. He kicks Jim, who doesn't respond. Eventually Jim joins in. Joe winds down like a gramophone. Jim trails off.*

Jim I'm hungry.

Joe I'm thirsty. I know that.

> *Pause.*

Eileen I kept him home from school. I had to. He's a bit feverish, I think.

Joe Why did she want to leave me? She left me, you know.

Jim She didn't, Joe.

Joe Didn't she? What was it then?

Jim She just wanted a break.

Joe Wanted a break. She wanted a break. What's that? Eh? She wanted a break. She wanted to read the *Manchester Guardian*. She wanted. What didn't she want? Wanted a break. That's all she did. Want a break. Broke me up, I can tell you that.

Eileen I had to put him up, Joe. He wasn't well.

Joe Did you?

Eileen Where have you been? As if I didn't know.

Joe Is there anything on my breath? Is there?

Eileen I wouldn't care if there was.

Joe And if I didn't come in earlier it's because he asked me to work on.

Eileen I'll do for you one of these days.

Joe That's nothing to what I'll do to you.

Eileen What'll you do?

Joe I'll think of something.

Eileen What'll you do?

Joe I'll set fucking fire to you.

Eileen Don't come near me, Joe. Don't touch me.

Joe I wouldn't touch you if I'd been inside for six months and you come in my slammer.

Eileen You bloody . . .

Joe It's your blood on the sheets.

Eileen I'll leave you, Joe. I will I'm telling you. Now I'm telling you.

Joe There's the door. You haven't got the guts.

Eileen I'd have to have guts to stay. But I'll go for good I will.

Joe And don't think I won't find out. I'll find out. I'll fucking find out.

Eileen What'll you find out?

Joe You know what I'll find out. And I'll put you out and I'll set fire to you.

Eileen I bet you will and all.

Joe I will. I will.

Eileen Stop it. Stop it, you'll wake him.

Joe Well, leave me alone then.

  Pause.

Did I kill her?

Joe You never killed her.

Jim Did you kill her?

Joe I never killed her.

Eileen I think that's him calling out. He must have woke up.

Joe I'm not surprised. Do you want me to go up?

Eileen I'd better go up.

Joe I'll go.

Eileen No I'll go. It's alright. (*She moves to the door.*)

Joe There was blood all over the shop.

  She stops.

Jim No there wasn't.

Joe All over the clothes.

Jim There wasn't.

Joe And the baby.

Jim There wasn't.

248

Joe And the oil-cloth and the chest and the mirror.

Jim There wasn't.

Joe And the sheets. They're full of it. Lumps of it. I lifted him out of it and . . .

Jim What?

Joe I took him down, then I took him in bed with me. Then they took her away.

Pause.

Someone will have to clean it up up there.

Eileen exits.

Jim What?

Joe What did she want to do that for? Eh? What did you want to leave us for?

Jim You left me.

Joe I didn't.

Jim Didn't you?

Joe I didn't send you back. They did.

Jim I wanted to stay when I come up. You never wanted me to stay.

Joe You crept in.

Jim I went to the dairy for her. I helped her. She liked me. She wanted me to stay.

Joe You pretended to be sick.

Jim You can talk – you were sick the night before exams. You were sick the night they put you away.

Joe You pretended to be sick in the enamel bucket.

249

Jim I was sick and I went to hospital but when I came out I had to go back. He took me back. It was raining. It had been raining for days. There was a fast black current of water covering the gravel and slate and the wide track above the house like the very beginnings of a catastrophe. She altered the blue shirt for me.

Joe She made that shirt for me.

Jim It was too small for you!

Joe They were sorry when I left school, and then when I wouldn't do a trade I disappointed them again. Then when I got into trouble it was the same. I'm sorry. No. Please. I'm sorry. I'm sorry.

Jim Get out.

Joe I was kissing you. Licking you. Who was hitting who? I didn't do anything. I didn't hardly even touch you. You was too young to come with me. There was blood all over the shop. All over your head. I'll have to clean it up up there. Oh kid. Oh kid. Oh kid. Oh Christ.

Jim Get out. GET OUT.

Joe Oh kid. When you were little. When you were little.

They are lying on the floor. The door opens. A boy of about nine years wearing pyjamas comes in. Leading Eileen. She's carrying another boy about two years younger, also wearing pyjamas. Half asleep, so that his face is hidden.

Eileen I've brought him down.

Pause.

Where are you both?

IN THE BLUE

In the Blue was first performed at a Studio Night in the Cottesloe auditorium of the National Theatre on 18 March 1985, and subsequently was included as part of the National Theatre Studio's Festival of New Plays at the Cottesloe in November 1985, with the following cast:

Stewart Ewan Stewart
Michael Michael Maloney

Directed by Peter Gill
Designed by Alison Chitty
Lighting designed by Laurence Clayton

Characters

Stewart

Michael

Suggestion of a room.
On the floor, books, clothes, magazines,
a towel, newspapers, records, tapes, a tray,
postcards, cups etc. Not too slovenly.
No furniture.

ONE

Stewart Right then.

Michael Are you going to ring?

Stewart I said I'd ring.

Michael But are you going to?

Stewart Yeah. Of course I am, what's the matter with you?

Michael I'd better give you the right number, then.

Stewart I've got it.

Michael No you haven't. Here.

Stewart Well fuck me.

Michael Yeah.

Stewart What you do that for? What a liberty. What you do that for? Fuck me.

Michael Haven't you ever done that?

Stewart No, I haven't got a phone. Anyway I wouldn't. Why did you do that?

Michael I don't know. In case you rang. I don't know.

Stewart But you asked me to ring.

Michael I know. Will you ring?

Stewart I dunno now.

Michael I thought you wouldn't.

Stewart I said I fucking would. Where's the number?

Michael Where's my pen. I can't find my pen. You got a pen? Thanks.

Stewart Honest. You. Honest.

Michael There we are. Thanks.

Stewart Right then.

Michael You off?

Stewart Yes.

Michael Are you going to ring?

Stewart I said I would.

Michael Or . . .

Stewart D'you want to leave it, then?

Michael If you want to.

Stewart Do you want to? Give me your number.

Michael Or perhaps . . .

Stewart Well . . . I'm off . . . I'll phone you . . . Shall I?

Michael Sorry? What? Oh, yes. You've got the number, have you?

Stewart Yes. Oh no. Where is it? What did I do with it?

Michael picks a scrap of paper from the floor and gives it to Stewart.

Oh yeah. Thanks. I'll see you then.

Michael Yes.

Stewart Thank you for the . . .

Michael Oh that's . . . Listen, ring first, OK? Don't . . .

Stewart No.

Michael It might be . . .

Stewart Yeah.

Michael You probably won't ring anyway.

Stewart What do you say that for? You never know. Do you? Eh? Anyway, thanks. OK?

Michael Yes.

Stewart And I'm sorry about the . . .

Michael Oh that's . . . Listen, take care.

Stewart Of what?

Michael I wonder if he'll ring. He might ring. He won't ring. Why should he ring? What if he rings?

Stewart Have you given me the wrong number?

Michael No.

Stewart Only I noticed the number when I came in. You gonna muck me about?

Michael Or . . . Do you want the number?

Stewart No.

Michael Or . . . Do you want the number?

Stewart No. Thanks.

Michael Or . . .

Stewart Here we are. OK?

Michael What's your name?

Stewart Stewart.

Michael You don't look like a Stewart. Do you charge?

Stewart What?

Michael You should charge. You've got the kind of flat and the kind of records. And you live in the kind of street.

Stewart What?

Michael It's so beautiful, this street.

Stewart What are you called?

Michael Stewart.

Stewart No. Come on. Come on.

Michael No. It's so beautiful, this street in this weather.

Stewart Is it? If you think so.

Michael I do. What are they, the trees?

Stewart Trees. Street trees. Are you a student?

Michael I wonder they haven't sold these off. These flats. These cold-water flats.

Stewart Why?

Michael They generally do. Sell them.

Stewart Oh yeah.

Michael They do. Do them up. Sell them. They do.

Stewart What do you mean, cold-water flats? This isn't a cold-water flat.

Michael That's what they are.

Stewart You're not in New York, you know. What *do* you do then?

Michael I like these flats up all those stone stairs. Do you have neighbours?

Stewart Why won't you tell me?

Michael I like the door knob, the broken glass.

Stewart Eh?

Michael This is just the kind of flat where the guy's on the game.

Stewart Do you want to pay?

Michael Yeah . . . Or . . .

Stewart I might see you then.

Michael Or . . .

Stewart Thanks.

Michael Or . . .

Stewart No. I'm not.

Michael Or . . .

Stewart Look at all these books.

Michael Or . . .

Stewart I'm off then.

Michael Or . . .

Stewart You read all these then, do you?

Michael Or . . .

Stewart Do you want to leave it then?

Michael Or . . .

Stewart D'you wanna leave it then?

Michael Or . . .

Stewart Do you wanna leave it then?

Michael I don't know, do you?

Stewart I don't mind, do you?

Michael I don't know, do you?

Stewart I don't mind, do you?

Michael I don't know. Or . . .

Stewart Shall I see you then?

Michael Perhaps.

Stewart See you then.

Michael Or . . .

Stewart I can see when you're excited.

Michael Or . . .

Stewart I've got plans for you.

Michael Or . . .

Stewart What are you into?

Michael I'm into you at the moment. What are you into?

Stewart Yeah.

Michael Or . . .

Stewart No I'm not.

Michael Or . . .

Stewart Are you scared? What are you scared of?

Michael Or it could be . . .

Stewart Ssh . . . ssh.

Michael What?

Stewart You'll wake him up.

Michael Who?

Stewart Lenny.

Michael Christ! Who's he?

Stewart The fella I share with.

Michael What?

Stewart Ssh, come on. He won't wake up. He won't mind if he does. He'll be quite happy.

Michael No.

Stewart Yeah! Come on.

Michael Or . . .

Stewart Right then!

Michael Oh yes!

Stewart I'm off then (*Pause.*) OK . . . (*Pause.*) OK . . .

Michael What? Oh yes. Yes. Or . . .

Stewart Do you want me to ring?

Michael Or . . . Why don't you ring?

Stewart No. I won't bother.

Michael Or . . .

Stewart Do you want to come in?

Michael Or . . .

Stewart Are we here then?

Michael Or . . .

Stewart This is it, then.

Michael Or . . .

Stewart Do you live by yourself?

Michael Or . . .

Stewart Mind the stairs.

Michael Or . . .

Stewart Is this all yours then?

Michael Or . . .

Stewart I don't want to hurt you.

Michael Or . . .

Slight pause.

Stewart Are you a student?

TWO

Michael I didn't think you'd ring.

Stewart I said I'd ring you.

Michael I know you did. I still didn't think you would Why should you? I wouldn't have.

Stewart Well, there's the difference between us, isn't it? I wouldn't have said I would ring if I wasn't going to ring.

Michael You didn't say much on the phone.

Stewart Wasn't much to say.

Michael You came round quick enough.

Stewart I didn't.

Michael Oh.

Stewart I took my time. Anyway, what's it matter? I wanted to come round.

Michael Good then, you're here.

Stewart Yeah, that's right. Well then.

Michael What?

Stewart Come here.

Michael No.

Stewart No, suit yourself. I can take my time. You still got all these books, then?

Michael Yeah.

Stewart *The Gift Relationship: from Human Blood to Social Policy*. When was that written? When the world was young? What have you been doing with yourself?

Michael Do you mean today?

Stewart Today, yesterday. What's the matter with you? Do you want me to go? I'm not going.

Michael Or . . . it could be . . .

Stewart I'm gasping for a fag. D'you smoke?

Michael I don't. I'm sorry. I know. Let's go and get some. Why don't you go and get some?

Stewart I'm skint.

Michael I've got money.

Stewart Let's go for a drink then.

Michael Oh.

Stewart Yeah! C'mon.

Michael OK.

Stewart D'you play pool? I'll teach you to play pool.

Michael I can play pool.

Stewart You can't play pool. Can you play pool?

Michael Of course. Can you?

Stewart Of course. I'm brilliant. I've kept myself in fags playing pool.

Michael Or it could be . . . What is it?

Stewart I think I've got something in my eye.

Michael Come here.

Stewart No.

Michael Pull your lid over it.

Stewart No.

Michael Go on. Now how is it?

Stewart I think it's better. Thanks. No, it's still there.

Michael Come here. Come here.

Stewart No.

Michael Come on. Hold still. There we are, look. There we are. OK?

Stewart Thanks.

Michael Or . . . Can you whistle?

Stewart Course I can whistle.

Michael You know, like this. Can you whistle like this? (*Demonstrates.*)

Stewart Of course I can.

Michael Go on then.

    Stewart attempts and fails.

I thought you couldn't.

Stewart What does that mean?

Michael Or . . .

Stewart How are you?

Michael Good, very good.

Stewart Good.

Michael I wish you hadn't asked that.

Stewart Why?

Michael Now I don't feel so good. I felt fine, now I feel fairly fucking terrible. Or . . . What if he keeps his cigarettes in his t-shirt? Oh my God. Or . . .

Stewart I came down two years ago.

Michael Or . . . More brutal exchanges, don't you think? Regardless of my views on the matter. Or . . .

Stewart I'm not living anywhere special.

Michael Or . . . Sometimes I think I'm as intelligent as I pretend to be. Or . . .

Stewart I came down with this young lassie. We travelled down together. After I got picked up by the police, she went back. I was bevvying a bit. No money. No kip. You couldn't blame her. I was sent down. I expect she's alright.

Michael Or . . .

Stewart I was in this doss in London and one morning I went to take a piss, and someone came in and said, where's Lenny and tried to kick the cubicle door in. So I went into the next cubicle and I pulled myself up to look about, and there he was, Lenny, sitting with his head rolled back and a needle beside him on the floor. Then the superintendent rang the police and said, he's dead as far as I can see. Take your time, anyway. He's no use to anyone. An old man died in the same doss, so the authorities came to take the body away. They handed him as far as the landing and one of them says 'Hey up' to the men below and tipped him over the banister. They never caught him. They put him in a box and carted him off.

Michael Or . . .

Stewart I like being with you. I do. D'you hear me? You. What about you? Hey.

Michael You're beautiful. I know that. Or . . . I thought of having my ears pierced.

Stewart That's a bit strong, isn't it?

Michael I should have thought it was a bit passé.

Stewart What?

Michael Old-fashioned.

Stewart It is.

Michael Then why did you have yours pierced?

Stewart It wasn't passé when I had it done.

Michael Who did it?

Stewart Lenny.

Michael How?

Stephen Stuck a needle through it. I'll do yours for you.

Michael No you won't. I'll get the charge nurse to do it with a suture needle. Or it could be . . .

Stewart What's that?

Michael A postcard from a friend of mine. He says we haven't seen each other for a year. And he says he's moving.

268

Stewart Where's he moving to?

Michael Tottenham.

Stewart That's nice. You'll be able to go for a holiday.

Michael He says the postcard looks like me.

Stewart Let's have a see. Who is it?

Michael Keats. It's not my fault we haven't seen each other for a year.

Stewart Who is he?

Michael We were in college together. We haven't seen each other for a year: must be a year since he got married. We were all in college together. I was the best man. I bought a suit. Humiliating, eh? It was like a footballer's wedding. Looked like a beer advert. Perhaps I should get married. Bastard.

Stewart Oh, I see.

Michael What?

Stewart Nothing, nothing.

Michael Or . . . Can't you get a job?

Stewart I don't want a job. I've had a job.

Michael I'm sorry. I'm sorry.

Stewart That's OK.

Michael I just meant. Well.

Stewart What?

Michael You seem . . .

Stewart What?

Michael I don't know. You're . . . Oh . . . Money . . . You're so . . . I want. Oh . . . Are you OK?

Stewart I'm OK. The giro'll do for me. I've had jobs.

Michael Or . . . What is it?

Stewart Nothing.

Michael You can tell me.

Stewart Nothing. I'm alright.

Michael Or . . . You're a lazy fucker.

Stewart Well you'd know.

Michael You take the action for the deed, that's your trouble. Or . . .

Stewart Look, Lenny was already on it. I don't do smack or anything much. I can take it or leave it. I'd rather have a drink, which is just as well on my income. What business is it of yours, anyway?

Michael Or . . .

Stewart Look?

Michael What?

Stewart Sweating.

Michael That's alright.

Stewart No it isn't. I don't like it.

Michael Come here.

Takes his hand and licks it.

Stewart You . . . (*Makes a fist at him, joking.*)

Michael Or it could be . . . then it could be . . . Or it could be . . .

Stewart Do you want me to stay?

Michael Or . . . it could be No. Or . . . No.

Stewart What's the matter?

Michael Or . . .

Stewart What is it?

Michael Or . . . No. Or . . .

Stewart It's alright.

Michael No.

Stewart Come on. Come on. What's the matter?

Michael No.

Stewart Come on.

Michael No.

Stewart What is it? What is it?

Michael How am I going to get through? A lot of people spend their lives just in drink . . . Don't have any afterwards. When you drop dead. Do you want everlasting life? Just got to grow old, when you come to think of it. Does that worry you? I think the problems start when you start listening to yourself. I know who I am but I don't know where I am. I'm all over the fucking place. This is awful. I could . . . Go away. I have to be by myself. If I could put myself in touch with my feelings I'd probably kill you. It's when you're not here I want you. I want to reach across and hold on to you. To hold you. Only I seem not to be allowed any feelings. I seem not to have feelings except sentimental ones. Or I seem only to have feelings. I seem to be all feelings. Don't, please. I'm frightened, I'm OK, I walk around and even now when I'm talking . . . If someone had died I'd have some reason for this. I'd have some right to this feeling. If you died. If someone had just died, even. If you were dead. But I haven't first call. You see . . . I think . . . You see, to dwell upon the ulterior motive for the sake of truth is . . . To over-emphasise that everything is dependent upon motive. To emphasize *that* truth is to deny that ulterior motive does not only produce results for the self. To think altruism is only worth measuring by ulterior motive is wrong. Stupid. Or to deny spontaneity. I'll have to get it together. How am I going to get it together?

Stewart You will.

Michael Do you think so?

Stewart You will.

Michael Never mind. I'm in pieces. Not even pieces, scraps. I'll have to get it together. How am I going to get it together?

Stewart You will.

Michael Do you think so? I don't think I ever will.

Stewart You will.

Michael Yet there's another part of me that doesn't give a fuck.

THREE

Stewart I've been for a drink.

Michael Good.

Stewart I've got to have a piss.

Michael Good.

Stewart I feel sick.

Michael Great.

Stewart Michael.

Michael What?

Stewart Michael.

  Michael goes to him.

Michael Sit down, come on.

Stewart No, it's alright, I'm alright thanks.

Michael You alright?

Stewart Yeah, you're a pal. I'm going for a piss, OK?
What's the matter?

Michael Now I feel sick.

Stewart No, don't feel sick.

Michael I think I'm going to be sick.

Stewart No you're not.

Michael How do you know I'm not going to be sick?

Stewart Are you gonna be sick? Michael. Don't be sick.
I'm not going to be sick. I'm never sick. Are you alright,
Michael? Oh, Michael, I'm going for a piss. You coming
for a piss? I feel rotten. Ah'm gonna put my fingers
down my throat.

Michael Now I feel really sick. Or . . . What is it?

Stewart Leave it, will you?

Michael Hang on. Hang on. Hang on!

Stewart Just leave it.

Michael What's the matter?

Stewart You are.

Michael Or . . .

Stewart I'm going for a drink.

Michael Oh yes.

Stewart Yes.

Michael Oh Christ!

Stewart Yes.

Michael Look, why don't you go for a drink?

Stewart I am going for a drink.

Michael Well go for a fucking drink then. Or . . . are we going to the pictures then?

Stewart I don't know.

Michael Well, do you want to go to the pictures?

Stewart I don't know, why should I have to make all the fucking decisions?

Michael Well why should I have to?

Stewart Well why should I?

Michael Don't shout.

Stewart I'll shout.

Pause.

Michael What is it?

Stewart I'm fucking confused, I can tell you. I've never felt like this before, I can tell you. About any fucker. (*Cries.*)

Michael Why? (*softly*) Why? (*Goes to him.*)

Stewart Get off. (*struggling*) You're so fucking clever you are, you ought to be done away with, you. You're sick. D'you know that? You're sick. You're sick, d'you

know that? You're sick. You are. You're really sick.
You're sick. You really are.

Michael Don't.

Stewart Do you love me? You love every fucker, you do.

Michael Come on. Come on, let's go to the pictures.
Come on. Or . . .

Stewart I have to thank you. No. I do. No, don't fuck
about. Thanks. Thanks. Hold still. Thanks.

Michael Or . . . Hello.

Stewart Don't start anything.

Michael Nice to see you.

Stewart Don't, Michael. Alright?

Michael Very nice.

Stephen I've put the kettle on.

Michael I've been everywhere looking for you. I've been
to the pub. I've been to the Irish pub. I've been to all the
snooker halls round here. I've been to Sid's Snooker
Saloon. 'You looking for Stewart? You've just missed
him.' I've been down Portobello to see if you were
scoring. I've been in the Elgin, I've been down All Saints
Road. I went over to Coldharbour Lane. All up the
Railton Road. I came back here again. I nearly rang the
law. I've had a really good time. You?

Stewart What you go over there for? I haven't been over
there. How long is it since I've been over there?

Michael I don't know. Where have you been?

Stewart Look, I was on the piss. I didn't think I'd better
come back.

Michael Where'd you end up?

Stewart I don't know.

Michael You know.

Stewart I don't. Look, it's none of your business where I've been, where I ended up.

Michael Just tell me.

Stewart I'm not telling you, Michael. And if you were so concerned, you should have shown some concern earlier. I can go out by my own if I want to, OK? Anyway, I asked you to come with me. I wanted you to come. I'm not staying here with you pulling me to pieces one minute and not talking to me the next. You talk about commitment. You haven't spoken to me for three days. What am I to do?

Michael Why didn't you ring up?

Stewart Because I didn't want to.

Michael I'll pull it on. I will one of these days.

Stewart Well you wanted me to go out. Didn't you, eh? Didn't you?

Michael I didn't.

Stewart Didn't you?

Michael I didn't.

Stewart Oh yeah? Well, why wouldn't you talk to me?

Michael Where were you, tell me? Please.

Stewart And anyway, what about you, eh? What about you?

Michael What?

Stewart You know.

Michael I don't know. What? There was an old man dying, I worked on.

Stewart You didn't tell me.

Michael Did you mind, then?

Stewart No, of course I don't mind. But you didn't tell me.

Michael You haven't said anything about it since.

Stewart Well, I'm saying it now. I had to ring to find out where you were.

Michael You didn't tell me.

Stewart To find out if you were working on. I had to make a right fool of myself.

Michael How was that making a fool of yourself?

Stewart Well, it was.

Michael Well, what do you think I was fucking doing last night? And I haven't been to sleep. And I've got to be up all tonight.

Stewart Now you know what it's like.

Michael Stewart, I worked all night because an old man was dying and they were short-handed and I spent most of the day with him and I worked on.

Stewart You're stupid, you are, anyway.

Michael What do you mean?

Stewart You're more qualified than what any of that poxy lot are. What's the matter with you! You've had an education. You give up a top job in the civil service and now you're a hospital fucking orderly.

Michael Auxiliary.

Stewart And how long's it gonna last?

Michael What?

Stewart What are you going to do next?

Michael What are you going on about? What am I
going to do next? What about you? What are you doing?
What do you do all day? Sleep, boozer, betting shop,
smoke dope, sleep.

Stewart But Michael, you haven't got the necessary to be
a tosser like me. What are you doing?

Michael Leave me alone.

Stewart But you're making a mess of yourself.

Michael I'm tired.

Stewart Why'd you give your first job up, eh?

Michael I don't know.

Stewart Why? Tell me.

Michael Don't. Please. Really.

Stewart Go on.

Michael I think I thought it was wrong. And you know
. . . Growth. (*laughing*) I wanted to do something
connected with people.

   Pause.

Where were you?

Stewart No.

Michael You've got to tell me.

Stewart I haven't.

Michael Tell me.

Stewart No.

Michael Alright. Put the kettle on.

Stewart It's on.

Michael Go on.

Stewart It's on, it's on. Do you want me to sing to you?

Laughter.

Michael Where were you?

Stewart You'll never find out.

Michael I will.

Stewart I doubt it. Got a paper?

Michael There.

Stewart Oh Christ, I've got to change. Have you got any clean underpants?

Michael I've stopped wearing them. They're bad for you.

Stewart Oh aye.

Michael Am I making the tea?

Stewart I don't know. Are you?

Michael Are you?

Stewart I will if you like.

Michael I'll do it. Where were you? Tell me.

Stewart Michael. No.

Michael Or . . .

Stewart I'm going.

Michael Why?

Stewart Ask yourself.

Michael Where will you go?

Stewart Don't worry about me.

Michael Or . . .

Stewart I don't know what I'm doing here.

Michael Don't you?

Stewart Cut it out, Michael, will you?

Michael Well, what did you say that for?

Stewart Because I don't.

Michael Why don't you?

Stewart I don't know.

Michael Why?

Stewart Stop it, Michael, will you?

Michael I don't think this is perhaps what we had in mind.

Stewart I didn't have anything in mind. I think it was you who had things in mind.

Michael Or . . .

Stewart I'm going.

Michael Don't do that.

Stewart No, I'm going.

Michael Where will you go?

Stewart Don't worry about me.

Michael I won't. Or . . .

Stewart This is stupid, this is.

Michael What is?

Stewart This is.

Michael Not as stupid as you. I can't do this. This is hopeless. You're so stupid.

Stewart Hey, you.

Michael What? What? I'm not scared of you.

Stewart Not yet you're not.

Michael What?

Stewart Alright. Alright.

Michael Or . . . I thought you were going.

Stewart I am going.

Michael I'm glad to hear it.

Stewart I am.

Michael Well go on then, fuck off then.

Stewart I will.

Michael I wish you would.

Stewart I will.

Michael Well go on! Go on! Why don't you just go! Or . . .

Stewart Right then! If that's the way you see it, you cunt, you're more of a soft prick than I took you for. Oh blimey, Charlie, shall I come over there?

Michael Oh Christ no!

Stewart I want to.

Michael Well I don't. This is like . . . I don't know what this is like. I wish I had the knack of taking opportunities. I can make opportunities. I'm great at making opportunities. Like . . . this is.

Stewart Don't, Michael.

Michael I'm alright. Don't come over. Or . . .

Stewart I'm moving out.

Michael Don't do that.

Stewart No. I'm going.

Michael Where will you go?

Stewart Don't worry about me.

Michael Why do you want to do that?

Stewart Why do you think?

Michael Or . . .

Stewart See, I can't handle it. I don't know what I'm up to.

Michael I see.

Stewart Can't you see what I mean?

Michael No.

Stewart Well, I'm not up to it. That's for sure.

Michael Or . . . What are you going to do about it?

Stewart What! About what?

Michael About me.

Stewart What about you?

Michael And you.

Stewart What about me?

Michael And me.

Stewart Cut it out, Michael, will you?

Michael I suppose one person can't be held responsible for the effect he has on another, wouldn't you say?

Stewart No, I wouldn't say. I bloody wouldn't say.

Michael Or . . .

Stewart I'll be off then. OK? Is it OK?

Michael What are you asking me for?

Stewart Well, come with me.

Michael Or . . .

Stewart Be nice Michael. Be nice.

Michael Or . . .

Stewart Why do you want me to go?

Michael I don't.

Stewart But you do, Michael, I'll go if you'll say.

Michael I don't.

Stewart You do.

Michael I don't! I don't! I don't!

Stewart You see.

Michael Or . . . Please.

Stewart No, for Christ's sake.

Michael I'll try.

Stewart No.

Michael I will.

Stewart You try.

Michael It's worse for me.

Stewart Oh yeah.

Michael I didn't mean it like that.

Stewart Oh.

Michael Don't go.

Stewart I've got to.

Michael It is possible.

Stewart I know.

Michael It basically seems to depend on whether you can do the washing-up. I'll do the washing-up.

Stewart Oh blimey. I haven't got it, Michael.

Michael Or . . .

Stewart Let's sort it out, shall we?

Michael Or . . . Or . . .

Stewart What do you want to do then?

Michael Or . . .

Stewart Am I staying?

Michael Or . . .

Stewart Come on, let's go.

Michael Or . . .

Stewart We'll be alright.

Michael Or . . .

Stewart What do you want?

Michael Or . . .

Stewart Just tell me!

Michael Or . . .

Stewart Why didn't you ring?

Michael Couldn't.

Stewart Who brought the letter?

Michael Me.

Stewart You?

Michael I didn't think you'd come.

Stewart Why, didn't you think I'd come?

Michael You're pretty diffident. Hence the note.

Stewart You should have rung me. Idiot. (*Laughs*.) Fool.

Michael You didn't ring me. But I'm grateful all the same. Thanks. Honest. Thanks for coming, thanks. Thanks.

Stewart How have you been?

Michael Fairly fucking dreadful.

Stewart Not so bad then.

Michael You?

Stewart Oh me. Of course. You know me.

Michael Don't you want to know?

Stewart What?

Michael Why the letter . . .

Stewart If you like.

Michael Listen, this is important.

Stewart I know, Michael. Honest, why do you think I've come over, eh? Oh Jesus, listen. There's more at stake for me, you know.

Michael Oh aye.

Stewart Because you'll eventually get fed up with all this. Bound to. And where will that leave me, eh? Can you answer me that? You alright?

Michael I'm alright. You alright?

Laughter.

Stewart I brought this back. (*Gives him a book.*)

Michael Did you like it?

Stewart Quite.

Michael I can't see why you couldn't have come round. What a bastard thing to do. Why don't you come round? I just can't bear the feeling that you're not coming round. That I'm not going to see you. But what would happen if you did come round? And yet there have been times in the last week when I have so wanted you to be here. Sitting here. When I've thought of things to say to you. Nothing much. Why? Why? But I'm no better than you, that's the truth of it. You'd better go, hadn't you?

Stewart I suppose.

Michael Hadn't you?

Stewart If you want me to.

Michael Will you be alright?

Stewart I'll be fine. I'll ring you.

Michael Will you?

Stewart I will. Honest.

Michael But, will you?

Stewart I said I would.

Michael You got the number. Where's the number? You got the number.

Stewart I've got the number.

Michael Where's the number? Oh Jesus.

Stewart Shall I ring you?

Michael If you want.

Stewart Do you want me to?

Michael If you like.

Stewart You've still got all these books then?

Michael Do you want to come in?

Stewart Shall we go then?

Michael What's your name?

Stewart Do you want a drink?

Michael Not very far.

Stewart By yourself?

Michael Not very often.

Stewart Where do you live?

Michael No. I don't.

Stewart Where's your jacket?

Michael I don't want to hurt you.

  Slight pause.

Stewart Are you a student?

Michael Or . . .

Stewart Michael, Michael, it's hurting, it's hurting.

Michael It's alright.

Stewart Michael.

Michael It's alright.

Stewart Michael.

Michael It's alright. Or . . .

Stewart Come on.

Michael No.

Stewart Yes. Come on. Come on. Come on!

Michael No.

Stewart Come on

Fight. Pause.

It's alright. It's alright.

Pause.

Do you want to leave it then?

MEAN TEARS

Mean Tears was first performed in the Cottesloe
auditorium of the National Theatre, London, on 22 July
1987, with the following cast:

Julian Bill Nighy
Stephen Karl Johnson
Paul Garry Cooper
Celia Hilary Dawson
Nell Emma Piper

Directed by Peter Gill
Designed by Alison Chitty
Lighting designed by Stephen Wentworth

Characters

Julian

Stephen

Paul

Celia

Nell

There should be an indication of Stephen's room
able to include other locations as indicated.

Scene divisions are not intended
to stem the flow of action.

Act One

ONE

Julian and Stephen.
  Julian reading and smoking. Stephen working at some papers.

Julian Listen.

  Stephen opens a letter with a knife.

Stephen Go on.

Julian
  'I never was attached to that great sect,
  Whose doctrine is that each one should select
  Out of the crowd a mistress or a friend,
  And all the rest, though fair and wise, commend
  To cold oblivion, though it is in the code
  Of modern morals, and the beaten road
  Which those poor slaves with weary footsteps tread,
  Who travel to their home among the dead
  By the broad highway of the world, and so
  With one chained friend, perhaps a jealous foe,
  The dreariest and the longest journey go.'

Isn't that great?

  Pause.

What would you say about me behind my back?

Stephen I wouldn't say anything behind your back.

Julian You wouldn't?

Stephen No, I wouldn't. Anything I'd say I'd say to your face.

Julian Oh yeah? Look at the bags under my eyes. Like what would you say? Is this shirt OK?

Stephen Yeah.

Julian It's not.

Stephen It is.

Julian But what would you say behind my back?

Stephen Stop it.

Julian My hair . . .

Stephen I'd say.

Julian What would you say?

Stephen I'd say. He's got nothing and he is everything.

Julian Fuck off, Stephen.

Stephen What?

Julian Fuck off.

Stephen What?

Julian Just fuck off.

   Pause.

I wish I could change.

Stephen Why should you change? You're alright as you are.

Julian But I want to change so how can you think I'm alright as I am? I should change.

Stephen I don't want you to change.

Julian You do.

Stephen No, fuck it. Give yourself . . .

Julian You wish me to change.

Stephen No.

Julian And I should change.

Pause.

I shall end up an old man in a hotel room.

Stephen For fuck's sake, you're young, young. Be young. Or you'll *always* just be young.

Pause.

Julian Stephen, why do you bother with me?

Stephen Julian.

Julian No, why?

Stephen You're my representative in the world of ball games.

Pause.

Julian Stephen. Are you making fun of me? Just tell me.

Stephen No.

Julian Are you laughing at me?

Stephen No.

Julian Really?

Stephen Look. You know I'm not. Why should I be?

Julian I just thought you might be.

Stephen Well, I'm not.

Pause.

Julian Stephen, I'm fond of you, you know. You're . . .

Stephen Last of the good guys, me.

Julian It's just, can't you . . .? No, forget it.

Stephen What?

Julian It's alright. Do you want a cup of tea?

Stephen Oh. Christ. Julian!

   Pause.

Julian I'm a horrible person. Do you think I've got glandular fever?

Stephen Yes. No.

   Pause.

Julian Fuck it. No cigarettes.

Stephen You're a terrible boy, you are.

Julian Am I? I'm not. Am I?

Stephen You're terrible! Here. (*He gives Julian two cigarettes.*)

Julian Two? Where'd you get them? You're great.

Stephen You're a bloody terrible boy.

Julian You really think I am, don't you?

   Long pause.

Stephen, do you think I shall ever get married?

Stephen Of course you will.

Julian I don't think I shall ever get married. I shall end up an old man in a hotel room.

   Pause.

Stephen Did you phone home?

Julian No. Yes.

Stephen What did you say?

Julian I said I was sorry.

Stephen What about?

Julian There was a row.

Stephen What about? When?

Julian Oh. Nothing, everything, the usual. Him. And them sending us away to school.

Stephen Yes, we're all victims of the class struggle.

Julian We fucking are.

Stephen Are we?

Julian Were you sent away to school?

Stephen No.

Julian At five? Half way across the world?

Stephen No.

Julian No.

Stephen That I *was* spared.

Julian Oh fuck off, you.

Stephen I *mean* it. Come on.

   Pause.

Julian Stephen.

Stephen What?

Julian It's . . . nothing.

Stephen What?

Julian Was it my fault?

Stephen How could it be your fault? It happened to you.

Julian I thought it was my fault. I thought he'd blame me. Dad. Not locking my front door.

Stephen But you locked the front door.

Julian I know. That's what started the row. I threw the table over. I'm fucking glad. Was it my fault?

Stephen How could it be your fault? It was you it happened to.

Julian I'm sorry.

Stephen Don't be sorry about it. There was a burglary. You were burgled. *You. You* were.

Julian Do you mind? Are you angry?

Stephen I'm not.

Julian You are.

Stephen Why should I be angry?

Julian It's the insurance.

Stephen Are you insured?

Julian Yes.

Stephen I'm not.

Julian My father insured me. I fucking hate him.

Stephen Come on, Julian.

Julian He gave me a briefcase with a combination lock for Christmas.

Stephen You're such a snob.

Julian Am I? I'm not. Am I?

Stephen Which of those alternative comedians were at university with you, Julian?

Julian None of them. I've told you those kind of people hated me.

Stephen Oh aye?

Julian They did.

Stephen Yes.

Julian They did, Stephen. You're such a bastard. Am I a snob?

Stephen Didn't you bonk or knob any of those girls who tell jokes about how they got thrush?

Julian Stephen. (*Laughs.*)

Stephen No, of course most of them went to Manchester, didn't they, or Sussex, or Bangor. The thing about your mob when they do comedy is they make you realise how funny Jimmy Tarbuck is.

Julian Well, I don't know of any Welsh humour of any sort.

Stephen No, and there are no fucking folk songs in the Welsh coalfields either.

Julian Yeah, and according to some sources there's no fucking coal either.

Stephen Ohowoho. You're the only uneconomic pit round here. Were you up with Manfred M . . .? No, before your time. Julian. Did you go to school with Mike D'Abo? No, no, no, no, no, no.

Julian You're so intolerant.

Stephen I don't know. I was very understanding when you said you liked Don't Look Now.

Pause.

Julian Stephen. Do you like the Velvet Underground?

Stephen Some of the Velvet Underground.

Julian So you know that song 'I'm Waiting for the Man'?

Stephen I know that song 'I'm Waiting for the Man'.

Julian That's a song about heroin.

Stephen Is it?

Julian sings 'I'm Waiting for the Man'.

Julian
I'm waiting for the man
Twenty-six dollars in my hand
Up to Lexington 125
This trick is dirty, more dead than alive.

Stephen Hey you.

Julian What? Alright. So I do heroin now and again.
I can handle it. I just got a touch of flu today. That's all.

Stephen Listen, Lord Althorp. I mean it.

Julian Would you?

Stephen Yes.

Julian Don't be stupid.

Stephen sings 'I'm Waiting for the Man', laughing.

No. You sound like Dylan. Do you like Dylan?

Stephen Bob, yes. (*Pause.*) Don't roll another joint.

Julian One more. Can I? Can I? Can I?

Stephen What do you mean, *can* you? You've already
rolled one.

Pause.

What are you doing? What? You're going to veg out in
front of the telly and watch one of your *Bilko* tapes? As
long as it's not *Hancock*.

Julian 'I'd be walking round with an empty arm.'

Stephen God, please, no, anything. Bruce Springsteen.

Julian begins to sing 'Born in the USA'. Another agonised noise from Stephen.

Julian Don't you even like Bowie?

Stephen He's about as lasting as Nelson Eddy, David Bowie.

Julian Who's Nelson Eddy? Don't you like anything at all?

Stephen Look, I like the band, I like The Kinks, Joe Cocker, Merle Haggard, Billie Holliday, Bessie Smith, George O'Dowd has a perfectly good voice, Cliff Richard has a perfectly good voice.

Julian Oh! Really!

Stephen Julian, I am not the rock critic for *Isis*. I am not interested in the irony of the Velvet Underground as perceived by . . . Terry Jones. Cliff Richard has a perfectly good voice.

Julian So has David Bowie.

Stephen Yes! I know. So has Nelson fucking Eddy.

Julian You're the most restrictive person I've ever met.

Slight pause.

Who's Nelson Eddy?

Stephen Ask your fucking father when next you have a row. 'This one's for Brian.'

Julian Don't.

Stephen
  'Life, like a dome of many-coloured glass,
  Stains the white radiance of the Universe.'

Pause.

Come on, Julian.

Pause.

Julian The worst time was having to go to bed at seven in the summer evenings with the light through the curtains. That was the worst time. The naughtiest boy was called Roebuck. I always think you're like Roebuck. He kept lizards in his pockets. And he hatched a bird from an egg he'd taken in the woods. They were always beating him for something or scrubbing him up to look angelic. And he never gave in.

Pause.

I don't know what I'd ever do without you. I think I'd just fall apart.

Pause.

Stephen, listen, do you think I've got a sense of humour?

Stephen Of course you have.

Julian No, honestly.

Stephen Yes. Tell me that joke.

Julian Shall I? I'm tired.

Stephen Come on.

Julian Do you mean when Roebuck said, 'Sir, what's the Latin for hinge?'

Laughter.

Stephen No.

Julian Well, when we were out, Roebuck and I, we used to find a telephone box, dial O and when the operator answered we used to say, 'Is that you, operator?' And she'd say, 'Yes,' and we'd say, 'Well, get off the line, there's a train coming.'

Laughter.

Oh, I hate it here.

Stephen What?

Julian England. I don't understand it. Let's go to Venice and Florence and Pisa, La Spezia and Viareggio and Leghorn and Rome.

Stephen Hang on, we haven't been to Lords yet. You said you'd take me to Lords.

Julian Would you like to go to Lords? It's great at Lords. We could spend the whole day there.

Stephen Alright. I've been to Rome.

Julian I've been to Florence. What does that matter? Did you go to the Baths of Caracalla? He wrote 'Prometheus Unbound' in the Baths of Caracalla. Are they beautiful? Listen.

Reads.

'This poem was chiefly written upon the mountainous ruins of the Baths of Caracalla, among the flowery glades, and thickets of odiferous blossoming trees, which are extended in ever winding labyrinths upon its immense platforms and dizzy arches suspended in the air. The bright blue sky of Rome, and the effect of the vigorous awakening spring in that divinest climate, and the new life with which it drenches the spirits even to intoxication, were the inspiration of this drama.'

Stephen Come on then.

Julian What?

Stephen Let's go.

Julian Stephen.

Stephen Where did he write 'Epipsychidion'?

Julian I don't know. Lerici, I suppose.

Stephen Let's go there then.

Julian I haven't got any money.

Stephen I've got money.

Julian No. I can't take your money.

Long pause.

Stephen You look at me as if I was fucking black magic, you know.

Julian sleeps, joint in hand. Paul enters.

Stephen Hello.

Paul You OK?

Tokes on Julian's joint Picks up book.

Who's reading this?

Stephen Fuck off.

Paul (*laughs*) Are you reading this?

Stephen Don't.

Paul Have you been sailing paper boats in the park?

Stephen Fuck off, Paul.

Paul gives the joint back to Julian. Julian wakes.

Julian Paul . . . is this shirt OK?

Paul Great. Where d'you get it?

Julian Do you like it?

Paul Great. See you later.

Points towards book, laughing.

Stephen Fuck off, Paul.

Paul So long.

Leaving.

Stephen Paul.

Paul What?

Stephen Fuck off.

Paul (*laughing*) Oh, Celia's downstairs.

Celia enters.

Celia Hello.

TWO

Julian and Celia.

Julian (*reading to Celia*)
'Meanwhile, we two will rise, and sit, and walk together,
Under the roof of blue Ionian weather,
And wander in the meadows or ascend
The mossy mountains where the blue heavens bend
With lightest winds, to touch their paramour
Or linger, where the pebble-paven shore,
Under the quick, faint kisses of the sea
Trembles and sparkles as with ecstasy . . .
And we will talk, until thought's melody
Becomes too sweet for utterance, and it die
In words, to live again in looks, which dart
With thrilling tone into the voiceless heart,
Harmonising silence without a sound . . .'

Isn't that great?

Celia (*looking at volume*) I wrote an essay on 'Epipsychidion' when I was at university but I never read it. There was a book out at the time. I cribbed it from that.

Julian *The Pursuit.*

Celia I think so.

Pause.

Julian Are you having lunch?

Celia I suppose so.

Julian Shall we have lunch together? Would you like that?

Celia Shouldn't we wait?

Julian I suppose we should.

Enter Paul and Nell. They all greet each other.

Paul Where's Stephen?

Julian Out, I should think.

Paul Where?

Julian He should be on his way back from the library.

Paul Shall we go and meet him?

Nell Yes, is it far?

Paul No.

Nell Shall we bicycle?

Paul No.

Nell Shall we see you?

Julian I expect so.

Nell See you then.

Paul and Nell go.

Julian I don't think Paul likes me.

Celia Paul!

Julian Fuck him.

Celia Is Nell a friend of Paul's?

Julian I don't know. Look. Come on. Let's go to lunch. I hate crowds, don't you?

Celia Alright. Where shall we go?

Julian I know a very nice place. Well, I think it's nice. Do you want to try it?

Celia Of course. Where is it?

Julian Holland Park.

Celia That'll be nice. Where? Oh! That . . . girl's name.

Julian Yes.

Celia Where are my keys? (*Julian finds them.*) What about Stephen?

Julian Fuck Stephen.

They start to leave.

Look, do you mind if I go and collect some blow first? You don't mind, do you?

Celia No.

Julian Do you?

Celia No.

Julian Celia. Listen, is this shirt OK?

Celia Yes.

Paul and Nell return.

Nell We gave up at the front door.

Paul Nell did. You off somewhere?

Julian Yes. Is that OK?

Paul What?

Julian Is it?

Celia Come along. Bye-bye, Paul.

They say goodbye. Celia and Julian exit.

Paul Here, take this. If I'm seen with *Private Eye* I'm in trouble.

Nell With whom?

Paul With myself. How long before you've got to go?

Nell Fairly soon.

Paul You always say that.

Nell Do I?

Paul You do. What is it?

Nell I've never been here before.

Paul Yes you have.

Nell Not here.

Paul How's Keith?

Nell He's fine, fine. He's fine.

Paul Is he in town? (*listening, calling*) Stephen!

Stephen enters, carrying books and papers.

Stephen Hello. Hello, Nell. Here. (*Gives Paul some magazines.*)

Paul Thanks.

Stephen They didn't have the *London Review of Books* so I got *Newsline*. He loves print. Newsprint. He's the only person I know who says he reads *City Limits* for the sport. Where's Julian?

Nell They've . . .

Paul Haven't seen him.

THREE

Julian and Stephen.

Julian Say.

Stephen No, I'm not saying. You work it out. Why should I come out with a lot of recriminations? You're happy. Off you go – have a drink – meet whoever – if you didn't want to meet me tonight you just had to say – now – go and meet whoever for whatever reason – you see now I'm doing it. What I didn't want to. I hate you for this. I do. If you apologise once more and don't even follow the apology through with something and then go on apologising I'll . . . I don't mind. I don't want you to change. I'll – I'll just wait for the time when I can say – why did I ever feel this about you? I look and watch and wait for you like a kid outside a pub sitting on the kerb or a step. Tired and waiting and still I wait. And I still wait. And I wait still. Look at the clock on the wall. But I haven't a time to expect you by. But twenty minutes have passed. I go back to my book to read something that makes me look up to see if you've come yet. The noise I've blocked out re-establishes. Glasses. Getting ready for the last haul before time is called. Phone at the other end. Singing has stopped. Clock. Don't look at faces – as I return one red-headed woman gesticulating imposes herself. Crisp packets crackle. Glasses again.

The noise is not unpleasant. Bit loud. I look up, I shall go. Leave you a note saying I've gone. Had you something more interesting? Wasn't there a half-promise? See you in the . . . I'll go. Not angry. Or shall I stay? Oh come on. Is it? No. I know you're not coming. I leave a polite note saying, you bastard.

Julian Look, I've got to go.

Stephen Where are you going? I'm sorry. I don't think anyone has ever been so cruel to me ever. So gratuitously. No. Yes. Cruel. They have been, I suppose. Ever. Not casually, culpably. Don't apologise. I can't think about it any more. I've managed to survive months of this, I've managed even to survive the redhead with the short stories. But I can't go on unprotected any longer.

Julian Stephen. Lindy! Stephen.

Stephen You told me you thought she was very nice. You told me you thought she was very talented.

Julian Did I? Oh God.

Stephen And then she sent *me* the manuscripts.

Julian I'm not worthy of you. Why don't you just give me up? I'm not worthy of you.

Stephen You've got some light. Some glow. I find myself crying and you know – I don't even know what it is I'm feeling. I don't know if I'm unhappy or not. I don't even fucking like you. I've located a part of myself in you. And I dread the feeling in the future of my sense of worthlessness now at having been so shallow all the time.

Julian But you can't let it be like this. Me!

Stephen Because there has to be a reason to get up in the morning. I have to have some defence.

Julian Against what?

Stephen That place.

Julian Where? Work? Against what?

Stephen The mendacity. The envy. The fear. The lack
of principle. The mismanagement, the lack of vision,
the self-interest. One's self-interest. The atmosphere
of witch hunt; the wish to make things worse. The
mishandling, the pusillanimity. The unkindness. The
lack of any care, the lack of guts to even stab Caesar
when he's dead. 'Speak hands for me.' The trivial nature,
the residue of complacency and dissatisfaction and graft.
The exhausted ideals, the lack of perspective, the dead
wood, the mediocrity, the vacillation, the meanness of
spirit, the gutless, not even opportunism. The terminal air.

Julian I can't go on with this. I can't go on talking
because you . . . such . . . You mustn't. I can't stand it,
I can't have it, do you understand? I'd like to bang my
head against a wall. If this is about Celia. If you're
quizzing me about Celia. There's nothing I can do about
it. Do you understand, do you understand? Do you
understand? You just want me to be infinitely flexible
and you resent my life. You do, Stephen. And you're
so very clever at making me feel obscurely guilty and
I *resent* it. I *resent* it. I'm tired. I haven't got the same
emotional stamina as you!

Stephen You selfish little bastard. It's not emotional
stamina. You're a coward. You're tired because you're
doped out and you're a coward.

Julian Leave me alone. I'm wrecked. I've got a headache.

Stephen You have no strength, you're a fucking coward.
It's weakness. You're just weak. 'Just give me some space
for a minute – space – give me space. I need space. You

don't allow me my space. I have to have space, OK'.
Sixties doped-out nonsense like that. Don't apologise –
you're like a drunk. And if you're going to get as stoned
as you were last night. There comes a point when one
can't have any more to say to you.

Julian Do you think you were sent by God to change
me? You make me feel guilty. Why do you look with
such reproach?

Stephen Don't you dare use the word reproachful to me
as a reproach. What you're saying is, if I look reproachful
you don't like it. I'll punish you. I'll hold it against you,
you say. I want something – you really can't give it.
You make me feel hopeless, hopeless, hopeless, hopeless,
hopeless, hopeless. What you're saying is, I'm tired,
Mummy. I'm tired. You perceive a look as a reproach.
You don't like reproach and you say I'm tired. I'm going
fucking mad. I hear something on the radio and I laugh
because it's going to be something I like and I think, got
you, you bastard. Then I feel the pain of wanting to
share it with you – pain that you wouldn't really want
to . . . and then I feel I can't sustain the hate – the feeling
current in me is too weak and the tears start and then,
to cap it all, before our next programme they play
Schubert's 'Seligkeit'. Do you remember when I was a
character witness over your driving offence? And I
thought in that awful court if I was in jail you'd forget
to come or come late. I'd look at the clock and five, ten,
fifteen minutes late you'd be. Then awkward. It will be
time to go. I used to like love songs. Now they have no
meaning. Sentimental songs have to be pretty good now.

Julian We don't ever have any fun any more. You're
depressed anyway. That's OK. Don't worry.

Stephen Well then, let's say goodbye. No. Come on. In
that case don't let's fuck about. Just tell me to fuck off.

Julian No. Come on, Stephen. Don't be stupid.

Stephen Shake hands with me. Come on.

Julian No.

Stephen We both seem to be determined to be ourselves to our mutual disadvantage. And let no one think they are protecting me by any hole-and-corner affair, when what they are protecting is something quite else.

Julian It's not you, it's . . .

Stephen The man Celia's going out with? That aging television man who irons his jeans?

Julian I feel I'm locked in a tennis court and people keep serving balls to me and I have to play and I can't compete.

Stephen But you do compete. You've put me in this tennis court.

Julian Look, this isn't flippant, she's captured my heart. Step, I think you only exist by hurting. Being hurt . . . I can talk.

Julian Look, I've got to go. Don't despair.

Stephen Despair? Despair! Despair's OK. It's anxious despair I don't like.

Julian I don't exist for you, Stephen, really. You'd like to blow me out.

Stephen Do you know, we don't know who the other is.

Julian I do. I know who you are.

Stephen But if what you say is true, and I expect it is. You're forgetting I *do* care! I honestly *do*!

Julian And me.

Stephen You're forgetting. Try as I can, I'm not as immoral as you are.

Julian Oh, don't moralise, Stephen.

Stephen Sorry. Sorry.

Julian Look, I've got to go. I'm really tired. And I've got to be up. I really have. I've got to get myself into shape. I've got to go for a run. Is it OK?

Stephen Don't give Celia my love.

FOUR

Celia with flowers in a pretty china jug.

Celia (*calling*) Are you alright, Julian?

    Pause.

These are lovely. Look how they've lasted.

    Pause.

Julian, have you seen Florence? (*listening*) Fine. Happy. Happy . . . (*Calls to her cats.*) Chloë . . . baby, baby . . . Florence . . .

FIVE

Stephen and Paul.
    Stephen drinking. Paul enters.

Paul What's this then?

Stephen I'm alright.

Paul What's this then? (*picking up a bottle of pills*) What are these? Where did you get these? OK?

Stephen Terrible.

Paul Is it?

Stephen It's terrible. Can I come into your bed?

Paul I expect so.

Stephen I'm going to kill him. I'm going to fucking kill him. I'll knife him. Please can I come in with you? Where can I get a shooter?

Paul What do you want a shooter for?

Stephen I'm going to shoot him.

Paul Oh. OK. But I don't know where you can get a shooter.

Stephen Someone must know.

Paul Nobody I know.

Stephen I'm going to kill him.

Paul What is it?

Stephen It's the anger. And the – anger. It's *terrible*.

Paul He takes up with a dislocated Liverpudlian who hit the hippie trail and who talks about Tibet and anarchy. He goes down West Indian clubs which he calls shebeens; plays pool in the George Canning. He can play two chords of 'The Wild Rover' on his guitar. He has the street wisdom of his mother's housekeeper. Why do you want to kill a figure of fun? He loves black music. Reggae. Ska. Scratch. Hip-hop. He really thinks, somehow, it brings black and white together. It's no different. Jazz. Rhythm'n'blues. Tamla Motown. People have always liked a black man with a banjo.

Stephen Don't be vulgar, Paul.

Paul Look. You can't . . . He may genuinely like the music, right? But these street acquaintances . . . The only reparation being made is to himself. And it does no good for him, with his nervous off-accent in a mini-cab to West Indian drivers who want honky out of the car as soon as possible. They still fucking hate in the same way I do. Look at the drugs. Look at the hypocrisy surrounding drugs. They say they're after the pushers. They only get the middle-men who depend on the Julians. The poor fucking . . . But they won't jail Julian.

Stephen You smoke dope, Paul.

Paul Yeah, I know.

Stephen Why are you so angry with him?

Paul I think perhaps because I'm jealous.

Stephen Why?

Paul I think I must hate something he stands for in you. Have you ever seen him spray his yucca? The yucca . . . And Shelley . . .? Whatever happened to Blake? They used to arrogate poor Blake in my day. Oh I don't know . . .

Stephen It's because in the beginning there was no one else in the frame. He knew no one. Because all this street acquaintanceship is so very touching. And because he was alone. Or rather he felt abandoned. He can't tell the difference between being alone and being abandoned.

Paul You mean *you* can't, Stephen.

Stephen It's the pure filament of self-obsession.

Paul Come on. He's not worth it.

Stephen What do you mean, he's not worth it? Of course he's not worth it. Who is worth it? Worth it. I know he's not worth it. He knows he's not worth it. And it's dawned on you he's not worth it. Worth it!
  He really doesn't have a life – he really is still only a string of appetites. Some of which he can satisfy. Oh, he's

weaker than I am. He has no, no, no, understanding of
other people. When he says he doesn't gossip, it's because
he doesn't have any interest in anyone. When he is
interested it's because someone has been kind to him.
He's like a light bulb. Lights up no matter who pulls the
switch. Stick with it, I say. Don't see him. Don't project
your future loss. But what am I going to do for the rest
of the evening?

He can't reciprocate even a desire for a friendship.
Although he seems to want to, and to an extent needs
to define himself by me. I even dislike him. He is callow
and yet sweet-natured – or, at least, what is charming
about him indicates sweetness and warmth. We went to
the Bacon exhibition. He can't bear human images. Bare
figures against a plain background. Couldn't understand.
What is it in Keats? He can't live without an irritable
reaching after fact and reason. Some of the figures he
understood, but he saw them as businessmen. Politicians.
Things to hate. Oh!

What's the opposite of negative capability? Positive
incapacity. I lack almost entirely that objectivity which is
supposed, by some, to be the prerequisite of being an
artist.

Paul Look, Steve . . .

Stephen I don't want a suitable love object. I just want
revenge on a couple of people, frankly. He's fucking
Celia. He's in love with Celia.

Paul Everyone's in love with Celia.

Stephen Are you in love with Celia?

Paul No.

Stephen You fucked her.

Paul I have not.

Stephen What's wrong with Celia? Ring this number. If Celia answers, put the phone down.

Paul It's an ansaphone. What does that mean?

Stephen Nothing. He sent her fucking flowers. Ring this number.

Paul Christ! Steve . . . No answer,

Stephen Oh . . . God. Roses. I think I was a very loving child and never grew out of it.

Paul Come on. Let's go down.

Stephen No, I'm OK.

SIX

Nell drying her hair.

Nell Darling!

Pause.

What time's your train?

Pause.

Keith, damn!

Her hair tangles.

Keith. What time's your train? Want a lift?

Pause.

OK.

SEVEN

Celia and Paul.

Paul Do you know what he's doing to himself?

Celia No. What do you mean?

Paul What do you think I mean? (*emptying pills violently on to the floor*) You live four streets away, Celia. He won't do anything but sleep.

Celia You know Stephen!

Paul Stephen? I know Stephen.

Celia Look, Paul, I'm sorry, he'll have to put up with it. I didn't mean that. Oh! He's alright, isn't he?

Paul Celia. I never thought you were stupid. What is it? You look as if this was the love of your life. Is it? I hope it is.

Celia Why?

Paul This smug radiance had better be worth it.

Celia Why?

Paul It's on the cards, I think. It really is. He's going to do something, Celia, only not, apparently, intentionally.

Celia But you're keeping an eye on him, aren't you?

Paul I never took you for a hard girl either. How is Golden Boy? Have you taught him to play bridge? I hope he's a better partner than you are.

Celia Paul. Stephen's, I owe . . .

Paul Your fucking job to Stephen.

Celia But Stephen's. Well, *you* know Stephen.

Paul Look, Celia. What are you saying? What? What?
I do know Stephen. What's Golden Boy think he's doing?
He's a real beauty, he is. A real fucking sleeping beauty.
He's like a dum-dum bullet, and what do you mean . . .
Oh, I'm going.

Celia Paul, I'm sorry, Paul. What about these, Paul?

Paul I'm leaving them for Golden Boy.

EIGHT

Stephen alone.
   Julian enters carrying a record set.

Stephen Hello.

Julian I've come to see you. Is it OK?

Stephen Yeah, yeah. How are you?

Julian I'm alright.

Stephen What's that – *Fidelio*! Julian! Where'd you get
it?

Julian Fuck off.

Stephen Sorry. Where'd you get it? Is this for me?

Julian No. Yes, it is for you.

Stephen Where did you get it? Did Celia give you this?

Julian Yes.

Stephen Yes. Her last boyfriend was a musician. I suppose
the next one will get a copy of the *Oxford Book of
Romantic Verse*. I'm sorry . . . I'm sorry.

Julian No, no, no, it's OK –

Stephen Are you staying?

Julian Can I?

Stephen Of course.

Julian For a bit, I'll have to go later. Is it alright?

Stephen Of course.

Julian Stephen, why haven't I seen you?

Stephen Julian!

Julian Why are you laughing? What did I say? What is it?

Stephen It's alright, it's alright.

Julian You know I don't care for her half as much as I care for you.

Stephen This is really fucking awful.

Julian What is?

Stephen It's just I can't bear the thought of someone knowing more about you than me.

Julian She doesn't know more about me than you, nobody knows more about me than you. I don't know more about me than you.

Stephen Why are you doing this?

Julian I don't know.

Stephen There's a pullover of yours in there.

Julian Is there?

Stephen I've been wearing it, do you mind?

Julian No.

Stephen Because it smells of you. Pathetic, isn't it? Have you seen *Fidelio*?

Julian No.

Stephen Have you listened to it?

Julian No.

Stephen Have you been to the opera?

Julian Yes.

Stephen What did you see?

Julian *Der Rosenkavalier.*

Stephen Did you like it?

Julian No.

Stephen Quite right. (*Whistles.*) 'Hab mir's gelobt, ihn lieb zu haben auf der richtigen Weis, daß ich selbst seine Lieb zu einer andern noch lieb hab! Hab mir freilich nicht gedacht, daß es so bald mir auferlegt sollt werden!'

 Julian sleeps.

Julian What's that?

Stephen *Rosenkavalier.*

Julian What's *Fidelio* about?

Stephen Well, there's . . .

Julian No. No, no. What's it about?

Stephen It's about freedom and constancy. You should know about that.

Julian What's *Der Rosenkavalier* about?

Stephen Julian! You've seen it.

Julian I know.

Stephen It's about nothing.

Julian Is it good?

Stephen Very good.

Julian Which is the best? Is *Fidelio very* good?

Stephen *Very, very* good.

Julian Yes, I thought it might be. I didn't like *Der Rosenkavalier*. I don't like the fucking opera, do you?

Stephen Yes. No. I dunno. I don't go. No.

Julian Is *Der Rosenkavalier* good?

Stephen Very good.

Julian I don't understand anything.

Stephen Come on.

Julian Stephen.

Stephen You'd better go.

Julian Stephen.

Stephen Shall I call you a cab?

Julian Yes, I'd better go.

Stephen You're such . . . There's a towel of yours in there as well, and half a bottle of JoJoba, and the Eucryl Smoker's, and a pair of swimming trunks, and a tube of Daktarin, and the African fucking honey, and the Eau du Portugal.

Julian That's OK.

Stephen And a packet of three with one to go.

Julian has left the recording of Fidelio.

NINE

Celia and Julian.

Celia Are you alright?

Julian Fine.

Celia What is it?

Julian I'm alright, honestly. You?

Celia Not very. Are we going?

Julian Don't you want to?

Celia Not really.

Julian Don't let's go then.

Pause.

What is it Cels? You've been like this for hours. What've I done?

Celia Nothing. Honestly. Let's stop. Let's stop it.

Julian Something . . .

Celia You can't accommodate to anybody, can you?

Julian What?

Celia Everybody must accommodate to you.

Julian What? Christ! Christ! What? To me? Who's been doing the accommodating if I haven't been doing the accommodating?

Celia Alright.

Julian It isn't alright. Oh no, it isn't alright. It isn't, alright. Oh no. Everything you want to do, I do. I meet your friends. I go to restaurants with people you like.

I go to concerts because you like them. I spend my time here. You haven't even visited my flat.

Celia I have.

Julian *Once.* My friends. All I did was not go to your parents, for the weekend. That's all, Celia. It isn't alright.

Celia I didn't mind you not coming for the weekend.

Julian You minded.

Celia I didn't. I'm perfectly satisfied with *my* parents. I can't help it if my father's a school inspector and my mother's a teacher. I can't help it if you don't like them.

Julian I don't know if I like them or if I dislike them, anyway. There's no reason for me to like them.

Celia Or dislike them.

Julian I don't. I don't know them. I don't want to know them. All this cosiness. I don't want to see them or visit them, or walk the dogs. Any of that nonsense. I don't want to know Mummy or Daddy. This is enough. Quite enough.

Celia Julian!

Julian Quite enough. Quite enough. Quite enough.

TEN

Stephen and Julian.

Stephen Will I see you later? Oh no.

Julian Why not?

Stephen You've got to have dinner with Celia, haven't you?

Julian That's tomorrow night.

Stephen It isn't.

Julian Isn't it? Where's her note? Christ, it is tonight. Oh God, I'm so tired. I think it's glandular fever. Stephen. Do you think? Listen, do you think I've got glandular fever? She says can we meet where no one can gawp. Really, who's interested in people gawping? Anyway, I'll have to go, won't I? Perhaps I'll just go for a drink. I'll ring her, we'll just go for a drink. What do you think? I'll have to have a shower.

Stephen Listen. I can't say anything. You go for a drink. I think there's something grotesque about this, anyway.

Julian Isn't this how you do these things?

Stephen I don't know.

Julian Oh Christ, I haven't got any money and I haven't got my cheque book. Do you think it matters?

Stephen No. Look, you'll have to pay. I've got thirty quid. Do you want it?

Julian Can I have twenty-five?

ELEVEN

Stephen and Julian.

Stephen What is it?

Julian Nothing.

Stephen What's the matter?

Julian Leave me alone.

Stephen What is it?

Julian I'm in trouble.

Stephen What trouble? Oh God.

Julian What? No.

Stephen What then?

Julian She gave me a lift home and when we got there she started crying.

Stephen Why?

Julian I asked her how the cats were.

Stephen How were they? Didn't one of them bite you once?

Julian Yes. Florence.

Stephen Christ.

Julian I made her come in, and we talked for hours and hours and hours and hours till two in the morning. She went home. Then I felt sorry for her and myself and went over there. What am I going to do now?

Stephen I don't know, Julian.

Julian She says she fought hard for her independence. Fuck her. I dreamt I was in a desert in America and you deserted me. I suppose you will. Won't you . . .?

TWELVE

Celia and Paul.

Celia It's when you can't change anything. I've tried, I've not been able to. I've only made it worse. Will you tell him for me, that he must or I'll die. How stupid, will you speak to him? Oh . . . Will you, please?

Paul Celia . . .

Celia No. He's . . .

Paul Yes. He's not much use to you, is he? Is he?

Celia He's left nothing. This for a little love. This for that. And yes . . . No. Oh I hope I never have to see him again. I do. I do. I do. I won't come out. Do you mind?

Paul Celia.

Celia I must go to work on Monday. I haven't been to work for two weeks. But I can't stay off any longer. I haven't seen anyone. Please, you won't tell him I've spoken to you, will you?

Paul Of course I won't. Come on, Celia.

Celia No. I'll stay in. Thanks. Thanks.

THIRTEEN

Julian and Stephen.

Julian You know that girl? That tall girl? I think she was flirting with me.

Stephen Don't. Please don't. Don't. By every bloody thing, don't.

Julian Why not? Why not? Can't I?

Stephen Look, she lives with a very nice bloke. Just don't.

Julian What's his name?

Stephen Keith. I've never met him.

Julian She asked me if I was having an affair with you.

Stephen Aye, she would. Are you? That's why she was flirting with you.

Julian Is it? Really, is it? Do you like her?

Stephen I don't really know her.

Julian It's alright. She won't like me, those kind of girls never do. What's she like?

Stephen She's a hockey-field Venus. Half good-looking like you. Grew too tall to be a dancer, I shouldn't wonder. They live in Cambridge in one of those big houses on the Chesterton Road and her aunt was Wittgenstein's doctor's receptionist, or north Oxford and their mother was an actress, but gave it up to have nine brutally concerned children. Or she lopes along Chiswick Mall, the daughter of a judge. And gives you pebbles or driftwood for Christmas. Trouble. Take a very long spoon. I bet she was at the Band Aid concert.

Julian She told me there's a very good double bill at the Rio in Dalston. And that restaurant on Newington Green.

Stephen Yes. I suppose the return match'll be at the Ritzy in Brixton.

Julian No. She's . . . Keith? She's a terrible flirt.

Pause.

Am I only half good-looking?

Act Two

ONE

Julian and Nell drinking white wine.

Julian (*reading*)
  'Our breath shall intermix, our bosoms bound,
  And our veins beat together; and our lips
  With other eloquence than words, eclipse
  The soul that burns between them, and the wells
  Which boil under our being's inmost cells,
  The fountains of our deepest life, shall be
  Confused in Passion's golden purity . . .
  We shall become the same, we shall be one
  Spirit within two frames . . .
  One hope within two wills, one will beneath
  Two overshadowing minds, one life, one death,
  One Heaven, one Hell, one immortality,
  And one annihilation . . .'

Isn't it great?

Nell It's like making love.

Julian Is it?

Nell Do you want some of this?

Julian Thanks.

Nell What is it?

Julian I'm restless.

Nell Oh.

Julian Not with you. I don't know what I'm doing.
Work. Everything. I'm a sort of displaced person. I feel
like some sort of refugee here.

Nell How? Come on. Because you were born abroad. Really?

Julian That, I suppose. A result of feeling that school was where they called home and home was in Malaya and now I don't know where I am.

Nell Why don't you go back?

Julian I'd like to. I'd love to.

Nell I've never been very far . . . Elba.

Julian Oh, Malaya . . . oh, you should.

Nell What are you laughing at?

Julian Thinking of here and there.

Nell Where were you born?

Julian Kuala Lumpur. But mainly I think of the Cameron Highlands house.

Nell Not a plantation? Really?

Julian Really.

Nell How very glamorous. I can see how you feel as you do. Though I like where we live. Where I was born, in fact.

Julian Where?

Nell North. On the Borders. There is something utterly strange and beautiful and compelling about Border Country, I think . . . I went to Wales once and we got to somewhere out of Shakespeare . . . Mortimer's Cross. And I got this feeling, scary. Beautiful. I expected Red Indians. But our Borders . . .

Julian Do you go home?

Nell I love going home. In spite of . . . Mainly for the place. The village. The town. Our house and when we're all together, I suppose.

Julian In spite of what? What does your father do?

Nell He's a doctor. He's a consultant, in fact. Mainly in Newcastle. But sometimes in Edinburgh and even London. But he won't move here. He likes the North and the Scots, though he's very English. We all went to boarding schools in the South and my brother went to public school here. You must come. My mother likes visitors and us all there. Though I don't like her very much.

Julian Why?

Nell Well, of course I do. But. What is it about Malaya? Is it like India? How they write about it. Is it like that?

Julian Yes. Longing. But it's everything, the people.

Nell Did you have an ayah? No, that's India.

Julian Yes, we had an amah. She was called an amah. My favourite had to leave – to go back to her village. It's just everything. The green. England! The green in Malaya. I'm sure where you live is beautiful. We used to go to Scotland. But there. Everything. The rain. I stood in the rain once and my parents were rowing inside. I ran off the verandah and into the rain. The rain was just soaking me. English rain is so hateful somehow. Mean. Untrustworthy. Cold.

Nell What did your father do before he retired?

Julian Not as romantic as you think, but yes, tea. After the war he worked for a company in Penang and then Kuala Lumpur. He met my mother there. They aren't grand, you know. My mother comes from Southampton.

Nell I'm sure there must be grand people even in Southampton.

Julian He was commissioned in the war. And then after was very hard-working and enterprising and clever and competitive.

Nell Was it his plantation?

Julian No. (*Laughs.*) He worked for a company. Later a huge American multinational company. He ended up Chairman of one of their subsidiaries back in Kuala Lumpur. He's loaded. I know he hates it here. More than me. He won't say. He was very big in the emergency. Not back in the army. But I don't know . . . being important . . . holding civilians together. Of course he thinks things have gone from bad to worse, which of course they have. Do you play Mahjong?

Nell What? No.

Julian My father and mother and their Sussex friends actually play Mahjong. He's, oh Christ, it's impossible. He's bright, I know he is. But he's so competitive. He knows the truth. I think he's lost his soul. My parents don't deserve a better chronicler than Somerset Maugham. They really don't.

Nell Are you like him?

Julian No, I'm not!

Nell Alright, angel, come on.

Julian I look like my mother. She's pretty despicable, I'm afraid. She's vain and weak and spoiled. Is that bad of me? His temper I have, I suppose. No, I don't. You?

Nell I can cope with my father, but I hate him for putting up with my mother. I hate her quite passionately really. Maybe because she'd had this man for years and my father knows. And her daunting competence I hate. I like my sisters and especially my brother, of course.

Julian What's he called?

Nell Giles.

Julian Do you want a smoke?

Nell Look, I should go.

Julian Don't go.

Nell Look, this isn't supposed to be on. I've got to see Keith before he leaves, though I'm fed up with him at the moment, actually.

Julian That's between you and Keith.

Nell Are you having an affair with Stephen?

Julian You keep asking that. Does it look like I am?

Nell Look, my brother's gay.

Julian So is mine. Or at least that's what he just told his wife.

Nell Giles, when he was at public school. I was always jealous of his romances.

Julian Really.

Nell He was once in love with someone called John Graham and he, John Graham, threw Giles over for someone called Philip Richards and Giles was so angry. So angry, he made himself ill, and he took two aspirins and was in the sanatorium for three days. He said it was my mother and I think it even was my mother. But it wasn't, it was John Graham. And that's how he got John Graham back. And when he, John Graham, left school, he came back during the term and took Giles out in his motor car. I thought it was incredible. I still do. Exciting.

Julian Not for Philip Richards, I should think. Do you want a smoke? Do you smoke?

Nell Sometimes.

Julian Have a smoke.

Nell OK – I'll ring Keith. Then I'll read something to you.

TWO

Stephen, Julian and Paul.

Julian I'm going out.

Stephen Don't go out. Come on. Sit down. What's the thing about one of your friends that you most like to remember?

Paul I don't know.

Stephen I know what it is about you.

Paul What?

Stephen In the other house I was sitting on the sofa by the fire, reading *Great Expectations*, and there was a soft tread on the step and a light tap on the door, and in you came and you said, 'Miss Barrett, Miss Barrett, I've come to take you away.'

Julian Look, I've got to go out.

Stephen Don't go out.

Julian I'm fucking going out to get some stuff, OK? OK, Paul?

Stephen Don't. Come on.

Julian exits.

Oh, Christ.

Paul A thing to hate. The public school as an image of England. They can take the slipper, these boys, but they don't know how to put their dukes up. And instead of going in the army where they belong, they persecute the rest of us.

Stephen Oh don't, Paul.

Paul I was in college with someone who went home at the end of the winter term and his parents had moved without leaving an address. There are families and families, Julian.

Stephen Young people are like unborn babies. It's the fate of each generation to have the young express themselves in different ways. Flappers. Teddy Boys. Flower children. Skinheads. And the old must put up with it. To me they look like unborn babies. Spoiled. I spoiled it. Seeking more. Not accepting the unfinished edge of things. Not letting it drift as it will. And put the effort in when it's needed. But why can't he say . . .? Why can't he show . . .?

Paul He can't because he's like that. And you'll have to put up with it or ship out.

Stephen What am I to do! I can't just drop him. I don't want to. Shall I give him up?

Paul Yes. And what will you do then? You're addicted to him. It's an addiction.

Stephen What do you know about Nell?

Paul When she left school she did something first. She didn't go to Cambridge straight away, I know. She wouldn't, I think. What was it? I don't think it was the VSO.

Stephen I bet it was VSO.

Paul Nor the National Youth Theatre.

Stephen It must have been one or the other. It must have been. I bet she played Helena. God, Vanessa Redgrave's got a lot to answer for, except perhaps her politics. Have you ever seen her? She's like a less subtly violent Nell. I bet Nell's shadowily concerned.

Paul I think she's fantastic. She burns me.

Stephen Who, Nell?

Paul No. Nell . . . Well . . . She has, Stephen, in her time.

Stephen But she isn't twenty-four any more.

Paul I'd give her one.

Stephen You've given her one.

Paul laughs.

Paul How was it at the weekend?

Stephen Home?

Paul Yeah. Your mother OK?

Stephen No. I think I'm too much bother for her now. I think my concern makes her even more agitated.

Paul Is she in for long this time?

Stephen I don't know. She just sits there and suddenly her eyes light up. I seem inevitably to be caught up in a passionate and romantic attachment for someone who needs you but doesn't want you. It's like an article in one of your magazines down there. The children on YOP schemes. Young boys joining the army. Brothers and brothers-in-law in and out of work. We went over to Cardiff for a meal. My younger sister, Kath, she's like a sans-culotte. We had to wait for a taxi for hours because she wouldn't go with the firm that took the

blacklegs to Merthyr Vale. She says they're killers by
implication.

Paul Aren't they?

Stephen My father says – 'I tell you, Stephen, I'm glad
I'm not a young man. It's worse than the thirties. I tell
you, Stephen, in 1926 when I was a shop steward' –
I never knew he was a shop steward, he never told me
he was a shop steward – 'we couldn't get two fellers to
come out on strike and we warned them, and when we
went back the manager sacked them.' He could have
only been twenty-four in '26. 'You in work, Stephen?
How's work? When you going back?'

Paul Yeah. Neurotic symptoms in the upper working
class. Routledge Kegan Paul. It comes to something
when your happiest times were when your mother went
to put flowers on her father's grave. Playing in the long
grass. Playing and watching. Pleasant, like another child
would watch its mother knitting. No tears. Sunny day.
Come here. There we are. Beautiful grasses. Secretly I
think my father would be relieved if I voted Tory. I think
it would be proof that I'd done something. But we seemed
to have moved class without breaking faith with chaos.

Stephen I don't know about my father – if I voted Tory
it would be the only thing that would bring my mother
out of the mental hospital. There was this play and a
man on a park bench and he said, 'I feel I haven't been
part of life.' Just like *The Cherry Orchard*. Something
like that. Have you been part of life?

Paul I don't know what that means.

Stephen It goes through one, I suppose in its own way.
If we will let life live us instead of being afraid or
thinking other lives should be our lives. It's our own life
we must live.

The new cruelties are the old ones, you know. The new respectability is just the grasping for individual freedom by a safe majority so they destroy individuals weaker than themselves.

The loneliness of all those people, lonely. They'd be less unhappy if they knew they were just lonely. Loneliness of the summer evenings of family life. The winter evening of after football. That rancorous mean-spirited arguing about sport. De-dum de-dum de-dum de-dum. Partick Thistle. Heart of Midlothian. Queen of the South. The loneliness not knowing it. The chocolate Swiss roll. My brother's football gear. My sisters arguing. Alone. Among them. Chewing gum under the table stuck to my trousers. Iron it out. The loneliness. Dusk, 4.30, winter. That sigh from her. That sigh. That snore from him.

Julian enters.

Julian Hello.

Stephen Alright?

Julian Yeah. Do you want some of this, Paul?

Paul Aye.

THREE

Julian and Stephen.

Stephen What is it?

Julian Nothing.

Stephen Fuck it, Julian. You were all over me half an hour ago. What is it?

Julian You're the last person I should tell.

Stephen Then if I'm the last person you should tell, why are you pulling this? When you look like this you're either dying or angry or frightened.

Julian Well, if I look like this why don't you take the hint and leave me alone?

Stephen Alright.

Julian I'm fucking furious.

Stephen Why?

Julian I can't, Stephen.

Stephen Oh Christ, why am I putting myself through this? I don't know what to do – is it a test? What is it? You make me feel nothing. I'm nothing. I'm so ashamed of this. Half an hour ago . . . This is wrong. Being with you makes me feel like a woman with none of the compensations, and I don't like it. This being controlled by a boy. Nobody can win with you, can they?

Julian I'm not competing.

Stephen You say I'm in competition with you. That's because if somebody puts an experience of theirs up against yours – then you think it somehow robs you. I'm not trying to. At least I don't think I am. Oh God.

Pause.

Come on, Julian.

Julian I asked her out and at the last minute she changed her mind.

Stephen Who? Oh God.

Julian She said she had to see Keith. Why did she do that?

Stephen Well, mm. Hang on. (*Moves away, hand to his mouth.*) It's alright. Oh, Julian. They do live together.

Julian Sometimes.

Stephen Well, I don't know. This is like being under the guillotine.

Julian Ah. Fuck it. I'm fed up with this. Nothing gonna come of this. It's alright, you're alright, we're alright. I'm going to ring her and tell her to fuck off. Oh, she won't be there.

Stephen Leave a message on her ansaphone.

Julian She hasn't got an ansaphone.

Stephen Of course she's got an ansaphone. All your girlfriends have ansaphones. They're like iron lungs to them. What colour are her eyes?

Julian Er . . .

Stephen What colour are my eyes? Don't look.

Julian Grey. I can talk about her mouth if you like.

Stephen I always knew you thought a woman's place was on her knees with a mouthful of cock.

Julian Stephen.

Stephen Julian.

Julian I wish I'd never met her. But I like her. She likes you.

Stephen Thanks.

Julian Do you like her?

Stephen I don't really know her. I can see why you like her.

Julian She's kind.

Stephen You mean she's classier than Celia. She won't make you feel so parvenu.

Julian Is she better than me?

Stephen Oh! No.

Julian Ah fuck her.

Stephen It's alright. (*Stephen exits.*)

Julian Stephen, is she better looking than me?

Stephen What? (*Stephen returns.*)

Julian It's alright.

Stephen It's alright. Sick. Here, this must be Nell's brooch. She left it in the bathroom.

FOUR

Nell chasing Julian.

Julian No no no. Here. (*giving her some flowers*) Don't.

Nell Thanks! Oh they're beautiful.

Julian Do you love me?

Nell What?

Julian I do.

   Nell laughs.

No!

Nell They're beautiful! Do you love me?

Julian With all my heart. You?

Nell 'I love you with so much of my heart that I have nothing left to give.'

Julian Where's that from?

Nell Aha! Got you! These really are beautiful. You have one.

Julian I can't carry a rose.

Nell Come on.

Julian No.

Nell Come on.

Julian No.

Nell Oh . . .

Julian Oh. What is it?

Nell I suppose we shouldn't . . .

Pause.

Stephen's in this, isn't he? Isn't he?

Julian No. Well, people are in everything, aren't they? Have you had a holiday?

Nell Yes.

Julian I haven't.

Nell Oh, poor boy.

Julian Don't.

Nell Come on. Oh!

Julian What? What is it?

Nell begins to cry.

Don't.

Goes to her.

Nell Don't. Keith's coming back. And then he's coming to town to live properly.

Julian That isn't a proper thing to discuss.

Nell Isn't it? Must we only discuss what you want to discuss?

Julian No. Don't be angry.

Nell Anyway, things will have to take their course.

Julian I'll wait, you know, for as long as it takes.

Nell Are we going to lunch?

Julian Yes. What . . . what are you doing this afternoon?

Nell Work.

Julian I'm damn well taking the afternoon off.

Nell That's rather irresponsible.

Julian Can you take the afternoon off?

Nell I *can* . . . but I won't.

Julian Come on. Come on.

Nell Haven't you had a holiday really?

Julian No. Where did you go?

Nell We went to Spain. Fantastic. What is it? Well, *we did* go. Where . . . where are you going?

Julian Oh. The Maldives or . . . I want to go to Italy. I was going with Stephen. He won't come.

Nell When?

Julian In a couple of weeks. I'm not going alone. I'm not going without you. Will you come?

346

Nell Alright.

Julian Will you? *Will* you? I'll get the tickets. I'll do the hotel. I know, I'll hire a car.

Nell Where?

Julian We'll fly to Pisa and drive to the Bay of Viareggio. It'll be great . . . (*Pause.*) What about . . .?

Nell I'll handle that. And Stephen?

Julian I've told you. Will you take the afternoon off?

Nell Wear this and I might. (*Gives him a rose.*)

FIVE

Paul and Stephen.

Paul Coming for a drink?

Stephen Aye. OK.

Paul Do you want to wait for Boy Blue?

Stephen No.

Paul We'll wait.

Stephen No.

Paul We'll wait.

Stephen No.

  Julian enters carrying a Paul Smith carrier bag.

Paul We don't have to wait.

Stephen We're going for a drink.

Julian No, I've got to pack.

347

Stephen Come for a pint.

Julian No. A pint. Oh no. Fuck it.

Stephen What is it?

Julian I've lost my driving licence. (*violently*) I've got an international bloody driver's licence and I don't know where it is!

Paul I'm going for a drink then, OK?

Stephen Hang on. Well, where can it be?

Julian I don't know.

Paul See you in the pub.

Stephen Hang on, Paul.

Julian I'll ring home, it may be there.

Paul So long.

Stephen Hang on. It'll be there.

Paul I'm going. (*Exits.*)

Stephen Paul!

Julian I don't want to go.

Stephen It'll be great. You'll meet people.

Julian Here. (*Gives him the bag.*)

Stephen What's . . . !

Julian You wanted it. (*Takes out a shirt.*)

Stephen What? Julian, the money.

Julian Do you like it? Do you? Do you really like it?

Stephen It's the most expensive shirt I've ever had.

Julian Do you really like it? Do you? Is it OK?

Stephen Great. I'll put it on.

Julian Oh Christ. I've got to go. I've got to go home for the weekend and then Gatwick on Monday. Oh God.

Stephen It'll be alright. Take them something.

Julian I've got something.

Stephen And keep your mouth shut.

Julian OK.

Stephen Hear me.

Julian Yeah.

Stephen Do you hear me?

Julian Alright. I'll ring you from the airport before the flight takes off.

Stephen You won't, Julian.

Julian I will.

Stephen How can you?

Julian I'll ring you.

Stephen Will you?

Julian I promise. I've got to go, OK?

Stephen Have a nice time.

Julian Shouldn't think so.

Stephen You will.

Julian Do you really like the shirt?

SIX

Celia and Stephen.

Stephen (*off*) He won't be long.

Celia Fine.

Stephen (*off*) He shouldn't be long.

Pause. Stephen enters with a tea tray.

Only teabags.

Celia That's fine.

Stephen pours tea.

Stephen He's usually in by now. Is that him? (*calling*) Paul! No.

Pause.

Work OK?

Celia Great. I've been promoted.

Stephen Really?

Celia Yes.

Stephen Paul didn't say.

Celia Paul doesn't know. That's partly why I came round.

Pause.

You look well, Stephen.

Stephen I am well. More?

Celia No. Thanks. No. Haven't finished this.

Stephen This is terrible tea.

She picks up a copy of The Face.

Celia Do you read *The Face*?

The Face is covering the recording of Fidelio.

Stephen No, I don't read *The Face*. This tea is really awful. Don't finish it. I'll make some more.

Celia No. Who's that?

Stephen (*listening*) Paul.

Paul Yeah.

Paul enters.

Stephen Where have you been?

Paul What do you mean, where have I been? To work is where I have been. Hello, stranger. OK?

Celia Hello.

Stephen She's been promoted.

Paul Have you? I'll get a cup.

Stephen No. Put the kettle on. This is awful. The water didn't boil.

Paul OK.

Stephen No, I'll do it. (*Stephen exits.*)

Celia Thank God you've come. I'll have to go.

Paul Why?

Celia Well.

Paul Julian? He's in Italy.

Celia Oh. With whom?

Paul Himself. Do you care?

Celia I don't. I don't, Paul. Honestly I don't.

Paul Anyone new? Going out with anyone?

Celia Paul. Yes, I am actually.

Paul Really, Celia. Your public secrecy. I'm glad about the job.

Celia Yes.

Stephen (*off*) I won't be long.

Celia Look. I'll have to go. I just wanted to tell you.

Stephen enters.

Stephen I made proper tea.

Paul This domesticity's a bit of a change.

Stephen Guests.

Celia None for me. I'm off.

Stephen Oh. Sure?

She kisses him. He returns the kiss. She starts to go. He stops her.

You look pretty today, Celia. Well, you always look pretty. But today especially. Must be the job.

Celia Yes. Bye. I'll let myself out.

Paul No.

Celia Really. Bye. (*Celia exits.*)

Stephen Do you want some tea?

Paul Yeah.

Stephen Pour it then, will you? I don't want any.

SEVEN

Julian and Stephen.

Julian Don't let's go on. It was awful really.

Stephen Come on. You look great. Was it really awful? No girls? No girls, Julian? What about the Grove of Catullus?

Julian Look, Stephen. Look, I can't. It just makes me nervous.

Stephen OK. You know you said you'd ring from the airport.

Julian Oh my God. When I got back? I didn't.

Stephen When you left.

Julian Did I? Oh . . .

Stephen Have you rung home?

Julian No. I haven't rung home.

Stephen Have you rung anyone?

Julian Do you mean Nell? Why should I ring Nell? Why shouldn't I ring Nell?

Stephen I don't know. Tell us about Italy, Julian.

Julian You know I'm not good with women. She's a friend. Just a friend. Can't I have a friend?

Stephen Why not? I've got a friend. Thank God for a friend. Thank God for Paul!

Julian Is he your best friend? Aren't I your best friend? I thought I was your best friend. Nell. I can't act normally as far as she's concerned. She's afraid she's going to hurt you. Celia said you have to get on with it.

Stephen Infatuation.

Julian What?

Stephen Look it up. Go on, look it up. You don't need to look it up. I looked it up. It doesn't help. 'Nativity once in the main of light crawls to maturity.' You're like the main of light. Angel. Isn't that what she calls you? Christ, Nell. 'While you've a Lucifer to light your fag, smile, boys, that's the style.'

Julian 'You're the most restrictive person I've ever met.' She calls me that. Yes. Why not?

Stephen Because, Golden Boy, it's so obvious.

Julian I've enough crowding inside my head. I've enough criticising myself. I don't need you crowding and criticising me. Don't say, look at that, look at that, listen to this. You're like, you're like . . . You're endlessly trying to describe me.

Stephen This is going to end up with one of us dead.

Julian You'll have friends if anything bad happens.

Stephen If you had a bit more character you'd have ended up a born-again Christian. I used to love you more than I hated you. Now I hate you. I hate you. Do you know I hate you? I've got to go through with this to learn never to do it again. Never. Never to let it happen to me again. I don't know what to do. You'll have to do something. I'm tired after work and I don't know what to do and it's all my fault, it's so humiliating. Why do I seem to be just letting this humiliation happen? I could kill you. Better than being dead. (*Pause.*) You really didn't like anything but the swimming and the food at all. Didn't you go into a church?

Julian Yes, we went into a church . . .

Stephen What is it? What's the matter, Julian?

Julian Nothing.

Stephen Was she Italian?

Julian I'll kill you if you go on about that holiday.

Stephen You'd be doing me the greatest of favours.

Julian Oh come on. You can't say that. Oh Christ. Don't say that.

Stephen Well. Where's the postcard?

Julian Would you like it? I didn't post it.

Gives postcard to Stephen.

Stephen But there's nothing on it.

Julian I was lying.

Stephen I don't care, write on it now.

Julian writes on the card.

There we are. Now I've got it.

Julian There was your card waiting. When I got in. Welcome home.

Stephen Look, don't make me feel bad for sending you a postcard because you didn't send me a postcard.

EIGHT

Stephen and Paul.

Stephen I wonder if he's taken her to lunch in Holland Park.

Paul Where in Holland Park?

Stephen A bar. Sounds like one of his girlfriends.

Paul I know.

Stephen Have you been there?

Paul No. What's it like?

Stephen It's like Bluebeard's castle.

Paul What?

Stephen I mean he takes all his serious attempts there. I spent a whole day there once.

Paul What's it like?

Stephen It's like a cross between a detoxicated opium den and the Copper Kettle. Moorish screens. Brass tables. Sofas. Dying palms. A dozing cat. Bits of church furniture. Ecclesiastical bric-a-brac. Bentwood chairs. Jacobean beams. Mock-Persian carpets stapled to the back of pews. Full of boys like him and girls like Nell.

Paul How do you know he's taken her there?

Stephen I know. The book matches'll turn up. You see, I know what things are going to be like. He didn't ring me. So I rang him at two-thirty.

Paul In the morning?

Stephen Yeah. I'm sorry. I'm sorry, he said. I put the phone down. Then later I made a transferred-charge call. So he'd think I was in a phone box. I heard him put the phone down. Then I got dressed and went out. It had been raining. I was cold. I went out to make a call from a phone box. So he could hear that sound, that infuriating sound before the money is inserted. And then let him know it was me and then put the phone down. But I didn't believe that the phone box *would* be out of

order as I had imagined. *Would* be broken, and the next,
and the next street. And that I would be walking the
streets in the wet until five in the morning and it would
be exactly as I had imagined. I went into the Casualty
Department at St Stephen's. 'I'm confused,' I said.
'Could you ring this number?' And they did. 'Are you
alright? Would you like to see a doctor?' 'No. I don't
exactly know where I am . . . could you just . . . here's
my phone book . . . ring this . . . no, *not* . . . *not* at that
number but at – oh, where is it? Here we are – at *this*
number – he'll be there and ask him to come and get
me.' 'Sit down. Have some tea.' 'No, I'm alright.
Actually, don't make that call. I'm in the driving seat
again. I just wanted to know if such help was available.
Thank you. Thank you. In case of emergency . . . such
as has just occurred.' And then I walked some more and
then another broken phone box somewhere behind
Olympia. And this young man was walking down the
street and he waited for me. What do you do? Do you
want a drink? I've just got off the bus. Where are you
going? Battersea. You're going the wrong way. He was
Scots. I thought I was hallucinating. The revenge was
too much. What do you do? Oh . . . You? I write stories
and poems. Bleak stories and poems I write. He was
thin. And I suppose drunk. I suppose. I couldn't tell. He
was soaked through. I didn't want it to happen. What's
the matter? I've had a row with someone. Oh, I've just
got off a bus. Where are we? Are you all right? Do you
know where you are? Aye. We were at home. Do you
want a drink? A Scotch? It's Irish. Aye. Shall we go to
bed? Aye. Do you want this drink? No. And then of
course. Suddenly. I don't like this. Where's the light gone?
I said, shall I put it out? It went out. I don't like this.
Are you alright? Yes, of course I'm alright. I don't
like this. What's the time it says? Five o'clock. I don't
like this, I'm married. What's the time? Five o'clock.

No, it's not. Yes, it is. It's my birthday. I'm twenty-six.
I'll have to go. I don't know what this is. Don't worry
about this. I'm not. Do you feel bad? Not at all. Not
at all. Where am I? Tell me where to go. You're miles
away. I've got to go. I so wanted him to go. But I tried
to persuade him to stay. His clothes were wet through.
I wasn't very convincing. It was a cashmere overcoat.
I got this in Brick Lane. Ten pounds it cost. I haven't any
money. You'd better stay. I'm depressed. The answer to
depression is suicide. Why are you depressed? The row.
I've got to go. What's going on? Will I get a bus? It's
quarter past five! Give me directions. We kissed. 'A fond
kiss.' He came from Glasgow. Why didn't I give him any
money? I had money. Why didn't I give it to him? He
was thin and poor. Tell me.

Paul I don't know.

NINE

Stephen and Julian.

Stephen Hello.

Julian Can I walk down with you?

Stephen Yeah. Yeah.

Julian It's nice to see you.

Stephen Mmm . . .

Julian It is. You don't know how nice it is.

Stephen Don't, please. I can't. Please.

Julian You haven't seen me for four weeks. It's nice to
see you.

358

Stephen Don't, Julian.

Julian is crying.

What's the matter?

Julian I can't bear it.

Stephen What?

Julian She won't see me now. I can't bear it, Stephen. Don't, someone'll see.

Stephen What does that matter?

Julian She won't see me.

Stephen Has she gone back to Dobbin?

Julian Mm . . . Keith. I think so. We did go to Italy together.

Stephen Ha! What? Ha!

Julian You knew.

Stephen I didn't know.

Julian You did know.

Stephen I really didn't know.

Julian You did know.

Stephen I really didn't know. I know now, though. It doesn't matter.

Pause.

That was a dirty bloody trick, you know.

Julian What could I do?

Stephen Not go.

Julian How could I not?

Stephen I bet the first coat you ever wore was reversible.

Julian Don't. I don't think I can bear it, Stephen.

Stephen Yes. It must be unbearable. Come on. Come on.

Julian No.

Stephen Why do I want this abasement?

Julian I don't know. You tell me. I don't want it.

Stephen What?

Julian What you said.

Stephen It's the thought of your prostituting intimacies. 'With all my heart.' I can hear you say it. Re-running conversations you've had with me. Do you know what it feels like to know a year of your life is being spunked over someone else on the beach at Lerici?

Julian Have I done this to punish myself?

Stephen You mean like a copy-cat murder? I dunno. I should think so . . . I still can't help loving the idea of you. The idea of something real in you. That was recently there in you. That is in you. Come on.

TEN

Stephen and Julian.

Stephen (*offering Julian a drink*) Here.

Julian No.

Stephen Go on.

Julian No.

Stephen Well, why did you come round?

Julian I don't know. Is it late?

360

Stephen Must be.

Julian How late?

Stephen Three . . .

Julian This is just a bundle of misery. Why is she doing it? Is she confused? Is she wicked? Fucking me over – like I've fucked you over. You can feel satisfied now.

Stephen No. I don't feel satisfied. I'm apprehensive. Yes. Of you. Again. But if you start anything. I warn you. I'll join straight in. You've taken all my sexuality and wasted it in . . . Nell. She's had me through you.

Julian I can't bear it.

Stephen Drink this then. Let's go to sleep.

Julian No. No.

Stephen You just reject everything I have to offer. The drink. The blanket. I don't do for you. And you have to reject even these comforts. You don't give anything. I only take by giving and you can't even take this. I can't get her for you. I can't go on being punished for this. Ring *her*. Punish *her*. Ring bloody Keith. Give *him* a basinful. Drink this.

Julian No. I'm going home. Thanks. I'm going to blow myself away. Perhaps that will satisfy everyone.

ELEVEN

Nell and Julian.

Nell Angel.

Julian I came hoping to see Keith, actually. Actually.

Nell Did you? Why should you want to see Keith?

Julian Because I did. Alright?

Nell If you try to see Keith, I'll never see you or speak to you again. Ever. *Do you understand?*

Julian Why are you doing this?

Nell What, doing what?

Julian Why did you ring me?

Nell Because I wanted to see you. I missed you.

Julian Did you?

Nell I'm sorry. I shouldn't have then.

Julian No. No. No. Listen, Nell. Listen.

Nell Yes.

Julian Listen, Nell. If you weren't with Keith, who would you be with?

Nell Oh dear. Don't be silly. You know.

Julian I don't know.

Nell You do.

Julian Honestly. Really. Really? Please.

Nell You know I can't.

Julian But it's over between you and Keith.

Nell Is it?

Julian I know it is. It can't be going to go on for ever. Not now.

Nell No. I can't see it lasting for ever. But you know . . . I love Keith.

Julian Stop it. Stop it.

Nell But you must know that I do.

Julian I don't want to hear.

Nell Well don't.

Julian (*pause*) And what about me?

Nell And you. And you.

Julian Please. I'll do anything. I'll wait.

Nell Angel.

Julian I will. I'll wait.

Nell Would you?

Julian I will. I've said I will, I'll wait until it's finished. You told me it was finished between you and Keith.

Nell When did I say that?

Julian In Italy, virtually . . . I'd just . . .

Nell What?

Julian I'd like to . . . again. I'd like to see your face change because of me. I saw it light up because of me. At the door. I just want to have that effect on you again. That's all. I just want to fuck you to see you change. Your eyes hollow and your skin and your mouth. Please, Nell.

Nell Look, Keith's coming back tomorrow.

Julian I don't care. Let me stay the night. Please.

Nell No.

Julian Then why did you ring? Are you mad or what?

Nell And if things are different between him and me, it's because of . . . this.

Julian What?

Nell Look, you'll have to go.

Julian No.

Nell Julian.

Julian No.

Nell Julian.

Julian No.

Nell Alright. Alright.

TWELVE

Nell and Paul.

Nell They call it an abortion. It's an abortion. My mother calls it an infection. A miscarriage is what it is usually known by. But it's a spontaneous abortion. I would have had a termination anyway. I don't want a baby. Anyway, I think probably I've got a slim chance, so they say. I suffer from cervical incompetence. I've got to have it done. I'm bleeding.

Paul Nell.

Nell I'm strong, you know.

Paul Are you? Where's Keith?

Nell He's coming down. He's been very kind. He's coming with me.

Paul Julian?

Nell He doesn't know . . . yes, I suppose it could be. What about Julian?

THIRTEEN

Stephen and Paul.

Stephen Tell me what to do, he said. Speak to her. I'll write. Don't write, speak. I rang her girlfriend.

Paul Who?

Stephen She says she never gave him any reason to hope. I can't understand what's going on in her mind. But I suppose third parties don't count in these matters. He spoke to her. Then rang asking me for a drink. When I arrived. He was . . . they were at the other end of the bar with that look of relief on his face that is his main reason for relating to people at all. I, *de trop* clearly. I went knowing he'd ring at eleven. He did. I didn't answer. He rang back at twelve-fifteen. I answer. He says, can I ring you back in a quarter of an hour? He had to go and see the man. He does dutifully. Ring. Christ. And doesn't want to speak. He's doped out and tired and full of hope. What on earth is she doing? I'm not sophisticated, you know.

Paul She wants the best of both worlds. Isn't that what we all want?

Stephen Really.

Paul Stephen, don't be such a kid. For Nell it's like the two-thirty at Newmarket. It's either Dobbin or Boy Blue. I think she's afraid of being thrown by Boy Blue. I give you six-to-four on Dobbin. Always excluding the possibility of a suitable outsider.

Stephen I think she says things – so he says – like, 'If we're fated to be together, we will be. No matter what happens I'll always love you.' Ghastly things like that.

Paul She's trying to draw it to a close.

Stephen Why?

Paul Well, she does owe Keith. And she does love him. And it must be faced, Stephen, that Keith must reach those parts of Nell that Julian doesn't get to.

Stephen They're getting a joint mortgage. Nell and Keith.

Paul No, they're not. A joint mortgage is the fashionable way of saying I do.

FOURTEEN

Paul and Julian.
  Paul reading a letter.

Paul 'Angel, the time has come . . .' I don't want to read this.

Julian Go on. Please. I don't know what to do, Paul. When I opened it and read 'the time has come' I thought . . .

Paul I could see you might. I really don't want to read it, Julian.

Julian I've told her I'll wait. Is she a bitch? Is she? Look, Paul, you know her. Tell me. Read it.

Paul 'I've never hurt so much . . .! No one has made me hurt so much!' Does she accept all the blame?

Julian Yes.

Paul (*laughs*) Yes. 'I'm sorry. My fault. No blame.' she certainly has a flowing pen . . . Ah . . .

Julian What?

Paul 'I only hope I have the strength of will not to see you again.' (*Reads more.*) Did you know she'd been in hospital before this?

Julian Yes. But not . . . it was mine. I know it.

Paul How do you know?

Julian Paul. You know. Because one knows.

Paul Does one?

Julian Yes.

Paul Have you shown this to anyone else? Have you shown this to Stephen?

Julian Yes.

Paul You've shown this to Stephen! Did he know about . . . before this?

Julian Yes. What am I going to do, Paul?

Paul What's the point of saying things like, if you don't watch out you're going to get into trouble one day? Nell, I know about. There's nothing to be said for Nell. Nell's what used to be called a free spirit. She's like Gwendolyn Harleth as seen by Rebecca West in a book which Virago found too dull to republish, 'Was she beautiful, or not beautiful?' It's Nell spelt with a 'K'.

Julian What do you know about Nell?

Paul You know there isn't any ownership involved. I know a lot about Nell. I even like Nell. I can still say I like her. I do. I have, and I do, and Stephen doesn't know and we have since you met and we have since you got back from Italy. But that's between me and Nell. Why didn't you keep this between you and Nell? What's Stephen done to you? He *isn't* your father, you know. You're going to get yourself into trouble. You are, sometime. It's no good saying anything to Nell. She's degenerate as far as personal feelings go.

FIFTEEN

Julian.

Julian I'm in purgatory. It lifts momentarily, and then I wonder. Why doesn't she ring? Then I think about Stephen . . . I know it was mine. I know. Dad. I hate Stephen. I'll ring him, he'll understand. Why doesn't he leave me alone? How could she do it? I'm going to ring her. I rang her. Ansaphone, ansaphone. She encompasses me. Why? She loves me. Why? Stephen. Why? Stephen. I rang him. I've got to go to bed, I say. Why? He rings back. I can't take him. I don't say anything. Why has she done this? I hate her. Dad. I hate him so much. I asked Stephen should I buy her flowers. I'm wrecked. Oh please, where is she? She's *fucked* me. And I'm in trouble with Stephen. Stephen. Why doesn't he leave me alone? I need to talk to him. He pisses me off. I'm not ringing Dad. I do hate him. Stephen's so fucking selfish. The rubbish he talks. I'm not seeing him. Fuck him. If he's angry, good. I'm fucking angry. Really fucking angry. Where is she? Why has she done this? Shall I ring her? I really hate her. Fuck them. I'm in torment. Where is she? I'm not ringing Stephen. What'll he do? Fuck him. Dad. I've put a message on her machine. I can't cope, I can't live without her. I hate her. I hate Stephen. Dad, I really *do hate.*

SIXTEEN

Stephen and Julian.

Stephen No.

Julian What?

Stephen She isn't better. She isn't more beautiful. She isn't cleverer. She isn't – than you. You're fighting her for possession of yourself.

Julian Yeah? I saw two people in the street just now, kissing, flirting, laughing. An ugly young man and a young woman looking much older than their age. She without teeth – he with bad teeth. Unkempt, dirty, drunk. Like children. Oblivious to everyone else. Why them? I've got nobody. Look, everyone is married. I'm losing her and you. Why do people tell you things and then not help you? I know she wants me really. I know.

Stephen Oh my dear, shall we never be able to . . . Shall you always be the thing you're . . . Shall you not want me? Shall we always be . . . Oh my dear, what a God-awful pity, eh? That people are suited and yet not suited. In rebellion. Struggling. You're like one's child. I can't desert you. This amidst all the welter of hate, envy, nerves, frustration. People will say you're very silly and spoilt – but they won't have seen the glimpses, will they? They won't. They'll perceive the charm. The looks. But they won't have seen you look ugly or have seen you when you've squeezed a few tears out. Or how bright you are or how painful your self-knowledge is. We colluded in a fantasy. We are colluding in a fantasy.

Julian She wants me. I know she does really. But she's too scared to leave him.

Stephen I'm like a dog scratching at the door.

Julian She is. She's . . .

Stephen I know she hasn't finished with you yet. I'm not certain you can honestly say you're finished with her. What if she arrives with her suitcases?

Julian I'd be glad of the opportunity to shut the door.

Stephen You wouldn't.

Julian What do you know what I'll do? Why do you
think you know everything about me? What do you
want?

Stephen Ownership of you is what I want, alright? OK?
Does that suit you? You want to say it too – say it to
someone as mediocre as you are. Someone you think of
as *really* mediocre, really. 'Is she better than me?' You
don't mean it. You think she's mediocre, which I don't
think of you really, you fucking, fucking bastard. I don't
think you even think that about her. Nell. Do you?
Yours is not as unhinged an obsession, is it? It's much
more acceptable. But you still want to say it – so's you
can say, 'I've suffered too. I've been fucked over, she's
fucked me over.' You're storing up things she's never
imagined, aren't you? To say to her eventually. But you
want her to fuck you over so you can say, 'I've paid. I
deserve worse in most instances, but in this one I've paid
for the others.' And when and if she says it's over *again*,
I'll be there. You've got right on your side, haven't you,
really? With all your pretence and free thinking, you're
right, you're right. The legacy of Romanticism . . . What
Lady Caroline Lamb said about Byron has lent glamour
to all the cheap irresponsibilities of people like you and
Nell ever since, without acknowledgement that Byron
actually produced something at least as substantial as all
the misery he must have caused. But you're so right. So
right. But even mad, red, rich, dead, not-very-cred
Shelley wasn't right on about everything. The avoidances
in *The Symposium* – what about them? Atheism,
freedom, feminism, free love – up to a point. But there
was something left to answer and there was no one
living whose ideas he could colonise in *that* respect.
What about the boy at Syon House? The Master at
Eton? Although, even after having written the coldest-

hearted poem any man could have written to his wife,
he at least saved her from dying from a miscarriage.
Something you would be too doped out or preoccupied
to cope with. What about Hogg and Trelawny and
Williams? I think it was a drowning of convenience.
I think there was something irreconcilable. You know
there's nothing intrinsically special about you. You
haven't earned this attitude by anything you've done –
except swim the mile. Your attitude is a result of money
spent on your quite inadequate education and your
inability to jump class with any grace. In spite of the
dope and the street-credibility, your mind is essentially
suburban. Nuclear fall-out. I love it. It's the only classless
thing there is. Do you know, I don't know whether or
not anything of what I've been saying has any basis in
truth at all. They were true words when I spoke them.
Or the feelings underpinning them were true. There
was feeling. But what I was saying. The opinions, the
rationalisations, I think they were just ways of trying to
say something else, really. I don't think what I'm saying
now is . . . I think it's genuine enough information. But
lies. I think. Not deliberate – don't have the words – or
am forbidden them. How can one just keep saying I love
you or I need you or I love you? Over and over. You'd
be bored. One has to say other things when one wants
not to speak at all but to say please or help or come or
love or please or cry. Over and over and over.

Julian Stephen. Do you remember once inviting me to
tell you to fuck off? Fuck off. Just fuck off.

*Stephen picks up the knife that he used to open a
letter in the first scene.*

Julian Christ. Stephen. Stephen.

Stephen Don't move. Paul! Paul! Don't move.

371

Paul enters.

Paul Stephen.

Stephen He's OK, it's OK. Don't you move. It's OK. Now see this. If I wanted to I could scar you in the only way that would matter to you. Look at me. I'm your mirror for the moment. Look at yourself. I could. It's alright. I'm not going to. Here, Paul. (*Gives the knife to Paul.*) Paul.

Paul Stephen.

Stephen He can't be loved. He won't be loved. Will you? You see, he won't be loved. You won't.

Paul Stephen.

Stephen No. (*to Julian*) Listen.

Little Boy Blue come blow up your horn
The sheep in the meadow, the cows in the corn
But where's the boy who looks after the sheep?
He's under the haystack fast asleep.

Pause.

Will I wake him? No, not I
For if I do he is sure to cry.

Isn't that great?